FLIGHT
THE HISTORY OF AVIATION

FLIGHT

THE HISTORY OF AVIATION

John Batchelor · Chris Chant

GALLERY BOOKS
An Imprint of W. H. Smith Publishers Inc.
112 Madison Avenue
New York City 10016

First published by Dragon's World 1990

This edition first published in the United
States in 1991 by Gallery Books, an
imprint of W.H. Smith Publishers, Inc.,
112 Madison Avenue, New York 10016

All rights reserved
Editor Diana Steedman
Designer Chris Harrison
Editorial Director Pippa Rubinstein

Gallery Books are available for bulk purchase for
sales promotions and premium use. For details write
or telephone the Manager of Special Sales, W.H.
Smith Publishers Inc., 112 Madison Avenue, New
York, New York 10016 (212) 532-6600

ISBN 0–8317–3380–2

Typeset by Bookworm Typesetting, Manchester

Printed in Singapore

CONTENTS

INTRODUCTION: THE PRECURSORS

The dream of flight is age old. Men have always imagined themselves cavorting among the clouds, wheeling and soaring like birds. In ancient times it was impossible to realize those dreams. People had to make do with mythical accounts of flying creatures like Pegasus, the winged horse, and gods like Mercury with wings on his ankles. There were even fables concerning manned flight like that of Daedalus and his ill-fated son Icarus.

The later Greek and Roman worlds were not particularly interested in technology, and appear to have had not even a minimal enthusiasm for manned flight. In the Dark Ages that followed, technology declined yet further. In any event the fragmented nature of society and the virtual loss of writing has left us with no records of aeronautical endeavours – in the unlikely event there were any. Gradually Europe began to emerge from this period in the ninth century, and in 852 AD it is recorded that Armen Firman, an Arab scientist, attempted a flight in Cordoba. History does not record what happened. After that, the Middle Ages is increasingly littered with vain and often fatal efforts to fly. These efforts frequently took the form of launch from a tower in a rudimentary glider or kite-like machine. The lack of any real understanding of aerodynamics and structures almost inevitably resulted in the collapse of the flying machine and the death of its occupant.

With the Renaissance, men began to reach a slightly better understanding of bird flight. This was in itself a dead end because man lacks the muscles to emulate bird flight and, at the time, there was no engine to provide the necessary power. Leonardo da Vinci and other far-sighted men produced interesting designs but these could never be translated into practical hardware, and the death toll climbed further as the castle and church towers of Europe continued to exercise their fascination for ambitious but foolhardy men.

However, it is worth recording that as early as the first half of the 15th century there were fully practical flying machines. These were not man-carrying aircraft but children's toy helicopters in which feathered or wooden blades were attached at an angle to a central hub. This was rotated by a drawstring, spinning the rotor and causing it to rise. These toys were probably inspired by windmills, but lack of motive power prevented development into manned machines.

But progress was made: Father Laurenco de Gusmáo probably flew a model aeroplane in 1709, and in 1783 the French Montgolfier brothers achieved the world's first manned flight in their hot air balloon. Ballooning, first with hot-air and then in hydrogen-filled balloons, became the rage, obscuring the single most important step in the evolution of heavier-than-air flight. In 1799, Sir George Cayley fixed the basic design of heavier-than-air craft in an engraving of a body surmounted by a large wing and trailed by cruciform tail surfaces for control of pitch and yaw, together with a diagram of the forces acting upon a flying machine. In the first years of the following century, Cayley moved forward with increasingly successful models. Then, after a lengthy interval, he experimented with manned gliders. The first flew in 1849 with a small boy aboard, the second in 1853 carrying Sir George's objecting coachman.

Cayley worked in something of a vacuum, but his ideas gradually gained currency with inventors. There were monumentally ambitious schemes by William Samuel Henson and others for steam-powered airliners, but more sensible men such as John Stringfellow remained content to explore aeronautics by means of increasingly sophisticated models. Two breakthroughs came in the 1880s. One was the invention of the internal combustion engine, which offered for the first time the possibility of considerable power at a useful power-to-weight ratio. The other was the poneering work of the German Otto Lilienthal in gliding. Before his death in an accident in 1896, Lilienthal had shown conclusively that sustained controlled flight was perfectly feasible. What was needed now was a combination of the internal combustion engine and a light airframe with lifting wings and controls.

Engraved on the front of a silver disc by Sir George Cayley in 1799 is a sketch for a fixed-wing aeroplane. On the reverse is a diagram of the forces of lift, drag and thrust acting on a flying body. From Sir George Cayley's Aeronautics 1796–1855, C. H. Gibbs-Smith, Science Museum.

CHAPTER ONE: THE WRIGHT BROTHERS

The men who finally achieved the goal of sustained and controlled flight were two American brothers, Orville and Wilbur Wright. Sons of the United Brethren Church bishop of Dayton, Ohio, the brothers were fascinated by flight, and in their business as bicycle manufacturers and traders were ideally placed to explore the technological ideas of others and produce their own developments. The Wrights took up where Lilienthal had left off. He had seen gliders as an essential step towards powered flight by teaching him the 'moods' of the air and how to control a flying machine in the air. Once this had been mastered, Lilienthal believed, an engine could be added to produce a practical aeroplane.

The Wrights followed a similar course but, inspired by the work of the American pioneer Octave Chanute, they opted not for the bird-like wings of the Lilienthal gliders but a more substantial biplane arrangement with interplane struts and bracing, together with a forward elevator. With hindsight, it is possible to see the forward elevator as a retrograde step. Rear-mounted control surfaces have become standard for most of the history of aviation. But it was adopted by the Wright brothers for the precise control it afforded their gliders, and for the fact that 'up elevator' would lift the nose from the ground rather than depress the tail toward it.

The Wright brothers also found the ideal spot for their flying experiments at Kitty Hawk, North Carolina. Here, on the Kill Devil Hills, an area of sand dunes offered the probability of soft landings and a useful elevation for launches. Steady winds helped their initial unpowered efforts. And it was isolated. The brothers were firmly convinced of the commercial value of powered flight and wished to complete their trials privately before patenting their machine and offering it for sale. The Wright Glider No. 1 was flown on the Kill Devil Hills as a kite in 1900. It was followed, in 1901, by the manned No. 2 Glider and, in 1902, by No. 3 Glider which had a rear fin for improved directional stability.

With the No. 3 Glider capable of sustained glides under full control, the Wrights decided that the next step was motive power. What they needed was a comparatively powerful engine of modest weight. In the absence of any such unit they designed and built their own, together with its twin two-blade propellers. These were located between the wings outboard of the centre section and driven by chains. One of the chains was crossed so that the propellers turned in opposite directions, avoiding the torque problems associated with two propellers turning in the same direction.

Towards the end of 1903 as the Wrights' accustomed flying season approached, the Flyer I was shipped to Kitty Hawk, assembled and its engine tested. On 14 December, the brothers tossed a coin to decide who should make the first attempt: Wilbur won. He climbed onto the lower

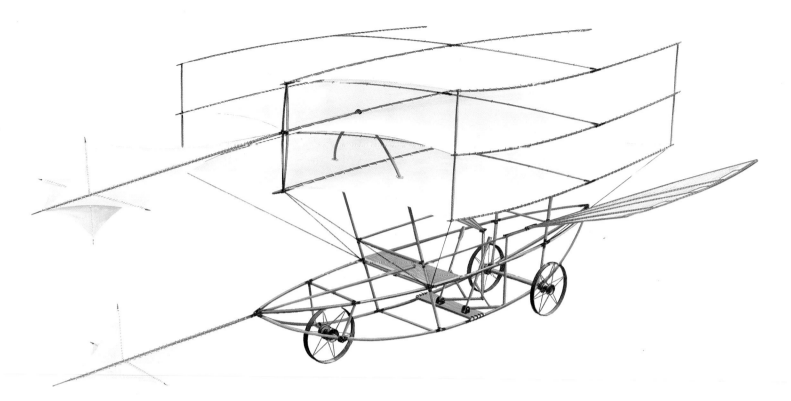

wing of the Flyer I, which rested on its 60-ft launching rail facing slightly downhill and into the wind. Wilbur gunned the engine. The aeroplane accelerated on the wheeled trolley, used as a launching device – the Flyer I was only equipped with skids. As the aeroplane lifted from the trolley, Wilbur put on too much up-elevator and the machine stalled into the soft sand. Repairs were carried out without undue delay, but the brothers had to wait until 17 December before the wind was again strong enough.

The launching rail was laid on level ground and facing into the wind, and with the witnesses and cameras ready Orville climbed aboard, ran up the engine and gave the signal for the tether rope to be released. The Flyer I accelerated along the rail, lifted from the trolley and flew for some 12 seconds, covering 120 ft before it touched down in the sand. It was the world's first true powered, sustained and controlled flight, or as Orville put it: 'the first in the history of the world in which a machine carrying a man had raised itself by its own power into the air in full flight, had sailed forward without reduction of speed, and had finally landed at a point as high as that from which it started'.

Three more flights followed on the same day, each improving on the last as the alternating brothers gained experience with the over-balanced forward elevator: the last covered 852 ft in 59 seconds. The elevator was damaged in the last landing, and Flyer I was wrecked just after the Wrights' assistants had brought it back to camp, when it was turned over by a gust of wind.

The first announcement of the Wrights' success was greeted with disbelief, and the brothers devoted 1904 and 1905 to producing not just a workable but a practical flying machine, tested at their new test ground, the Huffman Prairie at Simm's Station eight miles east of Dayton. With Flyer II, the Wrights made some 80 flights in 1904. Its take-off was aided by a weight dropped from a derrick attached via rope and pulleys to the Flyer II's lower wing. The best flight lasted more than 5 minutes and covered about 2.75 miles. And with their piloting skills honed in the Flyer

Perhaps the world's first 'successful' aeroplane was the 'boy-carrying' triplane glider designed and built by Sir George Cayley in 1849. This was tested in free flight with a payload of ballast, and then flown with a small boy on board.

Left: The brothers Wilbur (right) and Orville Wright, conquerors of the air.

Below: A side view of the Wright Flyer I at the Kill Devil Hills in 1903 reveals special design features such as the prone piloting position, the chain-driven propellers turning in opposite directions, the forward elevator and the twin rudders.

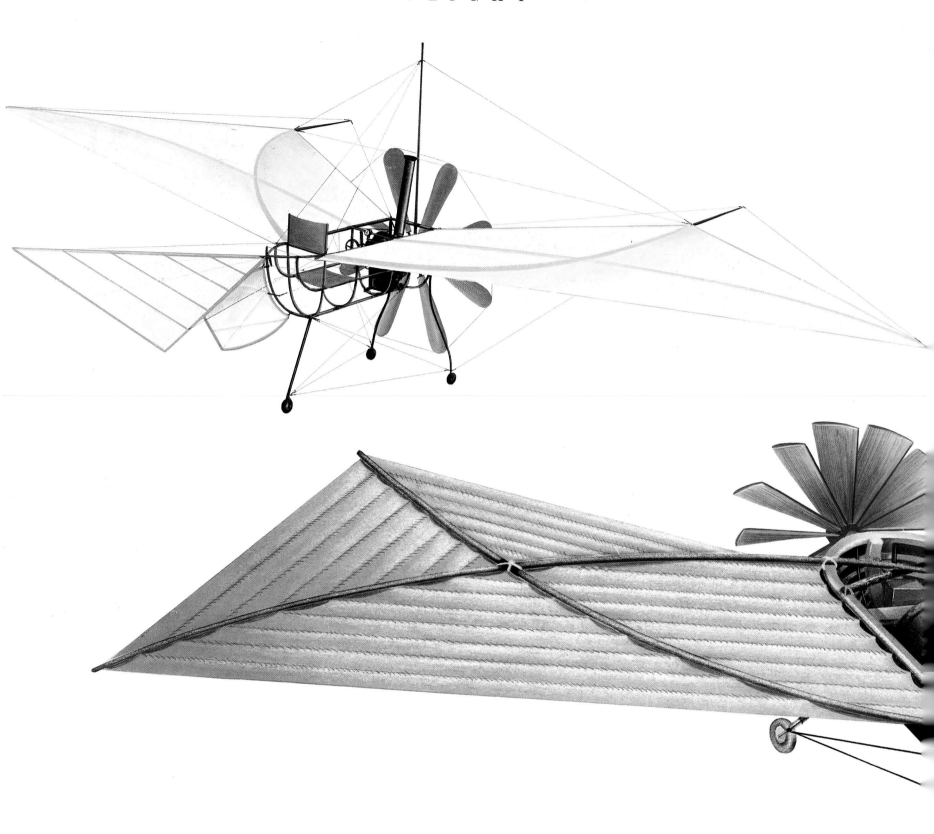

II, the brothers produced the Flyer III for the 1905 flying season. This was the world's first practical aeroplane, though it still used the assisted take-off device and, in the course of some 40 flights, recorded a best of 24.2 miles in 38 minutes 3 seconds.

At this point the Wrights ceased flying for a time. Word of their success was spreading and their patent had yet to be granted. The brothers now turned their attentions to the commercial exploitation of their Flyer. Between 16 October 1905 and 6 May 1908 neither Orville nor Wilbur took to the air.

In 1908, the brothers felt the time ripe to push forward with a demonstration of their capabilities. After some training flights in the Flyer III at Kitty Hawk, the brothers parted. Orville stayed in the USA to complete trials of the aeroplane ordered by the US Army while Wilbur travelled to France to exhibit the Wright A. The aeroplane was assembled near Le Mans in France, and on 8 August Wilbur astounded all those present with an amazing display of controlled and sustained flight. This far exceeded the first hop-flights achieved by Alberto Santos-Dumont in his 14-bis in 1906, which many Europeans claimed to have been the world's first true flight. As the pioneer Léon Delagrange put it: 'Eh bien,

Top: The first aeroplane to take-off (though only down a steep ramp) was Felix du Temple's steam-powered machine in about 1874.

Above: A graphic artwork reconstruction of the tractor monoplane design patented by du Temple in 1857. Among the advanced features of this unsuccessful type was retractable landing gear.

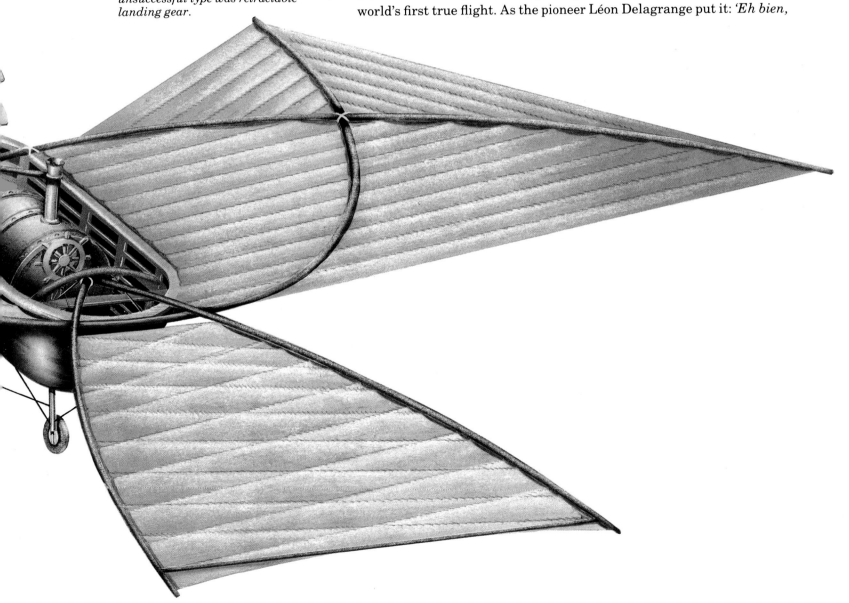

13

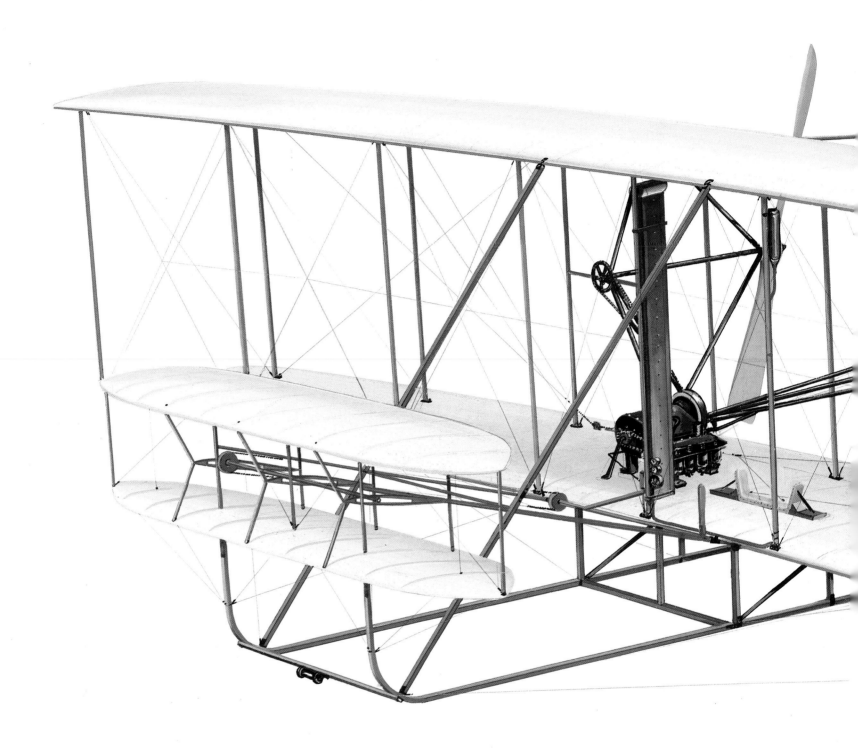

nous sommes battus! Nous n'existons pas!'. Later in the same year Wilbur confirmed the brothers' complete superiority over all rivals, both American and European, with a flight of 2 hours 20 minutes covering 77 miles, and another that reached a height of 360 ft.

Orders began to flood in for Wright machines, but from mid-1909 onward the impact of the Americans declined. As they sought to exploit their basic aeroplane with the establishment of flying schools and protect their commercial interests in a series of law cases, they failed to keep abreast of the developments their 1908 successes had spurred, and so faded from the technical lead at a time of extraordinarily rapid progress.

*The Wright Flyer I was the first
aeroplane that can truly be claimed as
successful in terms of taking off from
level ground before completing a
powered, controlled and sustained
flight prior to a landing on ground as
high as the take-off point.*

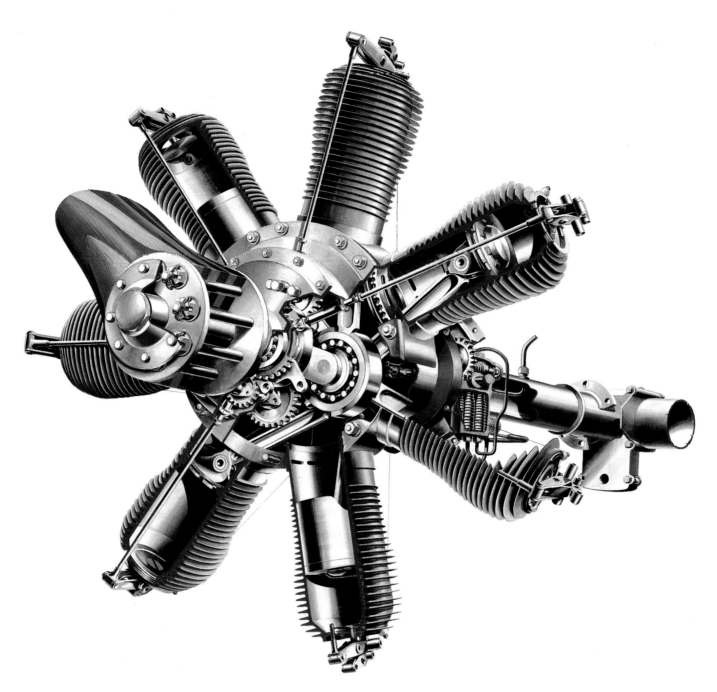

The engine that made practical flight a reality during the period leading up to World War I was the rotary. This was a light but modestly powerful type in which the crankshaft was bolted to the airframe and remained stationary while the cylinder block assembly, to which the propeller was attached, turned. This is an example of the Gnome-Rhône type of rotary used in the early part of World War I.

CHAPTER TWO: PRACTICAL FLYING MACHINES

The Maurice Farman M.F.7 was designed in 1913 as a reconnaissance and bomber aeroplane, but found its niche as a trainer. As a result of its forward elavator the type was dubbed the 'Longhorn' in British service, while its more conventional successor, the M.F.11 inevitably became the 'Shorthorn'.

Driven to furious activity by the example of Wilbur Wright in the second half of 1908, the Europeans responded with a flood of technical innovation as they sought to regain the lead they had fondly imagined was secure. Wilbur Wright's flights, impressive as much for their consistency as for their performance, pushed firmly into the background the achievements of European pioneers such as A.V. Roe and Samuel Cody in the UK, and Alberto Santos-Dumont, Ferdinand Ferber, Robert Esnault-Pelterie and the Voisin brothers in France.

The Europeans were swift to analyse the reasons for the success of the Wright A, yet they were not blinded by the success of Wilbur Wright and therefore sought to combine the best features of the Wright A with what was practical from their own designs. Licenced production of the Wright A was undertaken in several European countries to satisfy the demands of those who wanted to get into the air immediately, and there was a spate of Wright clones. But the pilot-constructors of the major European countries were further sighted and saw the practical disadvantages of the forward elevator, the lack of wheels and the reliance on the derrick launching system, the shoulder yoke to operate the wing-warping system of lateral control and the exposed pilot's position seated over the leading edge of the lower wing. These features lingered for a few years in some aircraft, but it is fair to say that from 1908 the Europeans appreciated their limitations and began to look for more viable alternatives.

The Europeans preferred the monoplane with the pilot comparatively safely ensconced in a fuselage cockpit, a nose-mounted engine driving a tractor propeller, wheeled landing gear (often in conjunction with a skid or skids to prevent the aeroplane from nosing over on landing and breaking the valuable propeller), a rear-mounted elevator (sometimes in conjunction with a nose-mounted unit), and ailerons for control in roll. These important and far-sighted features began to appear either individually or collectively in the large number of aircraft being designed or evolved from earlier machines. The level of aeronautical activity in Europe was immeasurably higher than in the USA, where only Glenn Curtiss offered realistic opposition to the Wrights and was embroiled in law suits brought by the brothers for his supposed infringements of their patents.

The speed with which the Europeans moved may be judged from their successes of 1909. The two most important of these were Louis Blériot's first heavier-than-air flight across the English Channel and the Reims aviation meeting. Blériot's flight on 25 July in his Blériot XI monoplane covered about 23.5 miles in 36.5 minutes and caught the imagination of the world. More important in overall results, though, was the Reims meeting of August. Some 38 machines were entered, and of these 23 (15 biplanes and eight monoplanes) of nine types (five biplane and four monoplane) got airborne during the eight-day meeting. The growing assurance of aviation is reflected in the fact that the 22 pilots who took to the air made more than 120 take-offs and completed 87 flights of more than 3 miles. The greatest distance covered in a single flight was 112 miles in just under 3 hours 5 minutes by Henry Farman in a biplane of his own design. The highest speed recorded was 47.8 mph by Blériot in a Blériot XII monoplane, with Glenn Curtiss only marginally slower in a biplane of his own design. The highest altitude reached was 508.5 ft by the elegant Antoinette VII monoplane.

Great publicity was given to the meeting in the European press. This resulted in a snowball effect of development as the pioneers saw the publicity given to successful flights as essential advertising for their aircraft. Just as significant, however, was the improved reliability displayed by the aircraft at Reims, showing that pilots could generally take-off when required and undertake the task imposed on them. There were of course accidents at Reims, but the positive aspects of the meeting far outweighed any negative effects of such failures.

The year 1909 can thus be taken to mark the emergence of aviation as a practical science. Though there continued to appear a large number of no-hope types – generally presented by their designers as the greatest aircraft ever produced – from this time forward the flying ability of heavier-than-air craft was no longer in question and the world began to consider aviation in terms of performance and reliability.

Right: Reconstruction of a World War I scene at an American air display as a replica of Werner Voss's Fokker Dr I triplane fighter makes a 'strafing' run on an 'Allied' airfield.

Below: The Blériot XI was the type in which Louis Blériot made the first heavier-than-air flight across the English Channel in July 1909. The feat produced a flood of orders, and Blériot XIs remained in service until 1915.

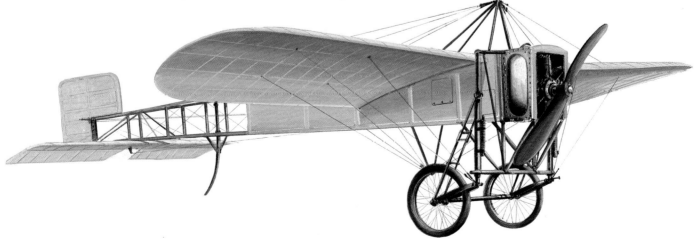

Nonetheless flight was still an adventure. It had no real practical application as yet, so the public emphasis was placed on race meetings and record attempts. These events were invaluable in pushing forward the technology of flying between 1909 and 1914. Aircraft were steadily upgraded in performance through the adoption of higher-powered engines in lower-drag structures. They were also improved in reliability by the adoption of the sturdier airframes made possible by the more powerful engines, and in safety by their stronger structures, more reliable engines and more refined aerodynamic design.

Aerodynamics were still poorly understood, it must be admitted, but

courageous pilots were pushing forward the frontiers as they attempted

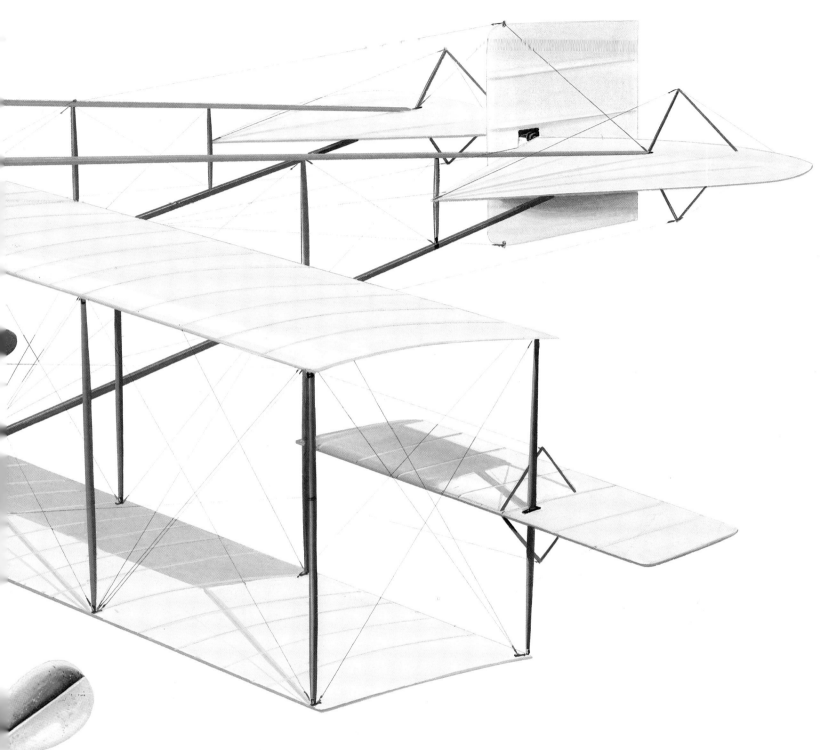

Bombing experiments were made in several countries before World War I, the most ambitious efforts being made in the USA with aircraft such as the Martin Senora and a number of Curtiss aircraft.

increasingly more daring aerobatics, and the mass of raw data being accumulated allowed more precise academic analyses to be made. But in the years up to World War I, the aeroplane showed a marked switch from the Wright type of pusher with a forward elevator and inherent lack of stability, requiring constant attention by the pilot, towards the layout that became conventional in World War I: a tapered fuselage located on wheeled (or float) landing gear and supporting biplane wings (with inset ailerons for roll control) and a tail unit with a rudder for directional control and elevators for pitch control. Though there were still several types of monoplane, emphasis was being placed increasingly on the biplane, whose wing cellule could be made very strong by the addition of bracing wires between the interplane struts and between the wings. Engines were also

21

forging ahead in power and reliability, the three most important types being the water-cooled inline, the air-cooled inline and the air-cooled rotary. The French were pre-eminent in the design of rotary engines, where the crankshaft is bolted to the airframe and remains stationary, the radially disposed cylinder unit and bolted-on propeller rotating around this fixed portion for maximum torque and cooling.

In the last years before World War I, the aeroplane also began to gain a purpose. This began with taking passengers for joy rides in larger aircraft. But soon there were trial services carrying lightweight freight such as mail and light bulbs. As the capabilities of aircraft improved, the far-sighted amongst the pioneers began to consider true air services between scheduled destinations, and in 1914 the world's first airline was established to fly passengers across the mouth of a large bay in western Florida. Progress with the airline concept led to many airliner schemes, culminating in the design of the world's first four-engined airliner, the Sikorsky Bolshoi, which flew in 1913.

But darker clouds lined the horizons, and considerable experimentation had already taken place with the arming of aircraft. The aeroplane was first used in war over Libya during the Italians' 1911-12 operations against the Turks. Though reconnaissance was their primary task, several aircraft had dropped make-shift bombs. Other nations were also considering bombing from aircraft, and experiments arming aircraft with machine-guns were tried with mixed results.

Like the B.E.2, the Aviatik B-series observation aircraft stemmed from pre-war thinking and located the observer in the front cockpit without armament.

CHAPTER THREE: WORLD WAR I

The air arms that entered World War I in August 1914 were generally small, equipped with a fairly heterogeneous assortment of aircraft, and with no clear tactical doctrine. On the Western Front, for example, the Germans fielded some 180 aircraft at the beginning of the war to their opponents' 208 (48 British, 24 Belgian and 136 French). Squadrons were rarely constituted with only a single type of plane. This made servicing a nightmare and co-ordinated operations all but impossible because the aircraft had such different performance levels.

However, aircraft achieved important results even in the first few weeks of the war. Though aircraft could carry no worthwhile load other than their crews of one or two, this was sufficient for visual reconnaissance. It was just such airborne reconnaissance that warned the Allies of the inward shift of the Germans' extreme right-flank army so that it would pass to the east of Paris rather than the west as ordained in the Schlieffen Plan. The Allies rearranged their forces accordingly and checked the Germans in the 1st Battle of the Marne, the first German reverse of the war. From this auspicious start aerial reconnaissance went from strength to strength. Soon cameras were carried. This was a vital tool in the mapping of the trench systems that sprang up between the North Sea and the Swiss frontier from November 1914.

Closely allied to reconnaissance was artillery observation. The orbiting aircraft spotted the fall of their guns' fire and sent back corrections: initially this was done by dropping messages, but later radio was used.

The standard British reconnaissance and artillery observation aeroplane in the first years of World War I was the Royal Aircraft Factory B.E.2, designed before the war as an inherently stable aeroplane. The B.E.2 was built in large numbers but suffered heavy losses because its stability inhibited the type of manoeuvrability that would have given it a chance to avoid fighter attack.

Both sides soon appreciated how important reconnaissance and artillery observation aircraft were. Gradually they realized that what was valuable to your own side was also valuable to the other. It was therefore useful to prevent the enemy's effective use of such aircraft – so the fighter was born. Initially the more aggressive pilots took up service weapons such as rifles and pistols, or even sporting guns, to pot at the enemy. There were also attempts to drop grenades or boxes of darts onto enemy aircraft, or to grapple their propellers with a hook on the end of a length of rope. Some Russian pilots even rammed their enemies, hoping that such an encounter would leave enough of their own aircraft to get down safely.

Machine-guns offered greater firepower and gradually found their way onto aircraft. The obvious mount for such a weapon was the two-man general-purpose aeroplane where the observer could man the gun while the pilot flew the machine. The only trouble was that in the early types the observer often occupied the front seat. This was bad enough from the reconnaissance point of view. His field of vision was poor, obstructed by struts and wires. But in the armed role it was worse. The struts and wires hindered movement of the gun and could easily be shot away by an ill-advised burst of fire. In later reconnaissance and observation aircraft the pilot occupied the front seat and the observer/gunner the rear seat where he had cleared fields of vision and fire.

But a slow two-seater is not the best machine with which to chase and engage another slow two-seater. There were already in existence fast single-seat scouts such as the Bristol Scout, Morane-Saulnier Types L and N and Sopwith Tabloid. With suitable armour these would make good armed pursuit aircraft. A trainable gun in such an aeroplane presented the pilot with insurmountable problems – he needs both hands to pilot the plane. The answer lay in fixing the gun to fire along the line of flight so that the pilot had merely to aim his aeroplane at the target and fire. The difficulty with this system was that the whirling propeller of these fast scouts lay between the gun and the target, and was likely to be shot away.

The French Morane-Saulnier company had already started work on a mechanism to interrupt the machine-gun's fire when a propeller blade was in line with the muzzle, but because of difficulties with hang-fire and cook-off rounds the rear of the blades were fitted with wedge-shaped steel deflectors. There were delays in finalizing this gear so the French pilot Roland Garros decided to fly with just the deflector plates fitted to the propeller of his Type L, and on 1 April 1915 he shot down a German aeroplane that was taken completely unawares by Garros's head-on

Above: The Lohner B I is typical of unarmed observation aircraft early in World War I.

Below: Italy was a major exponent of the strategic bomber, using Caproni aircraft. This is a Ca 2 (company designation Ca 32) with three 100-hp engines located as one pusher and two tractor units.

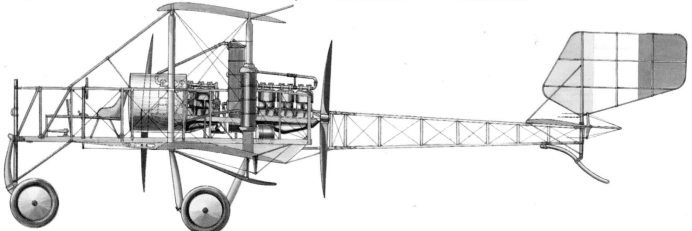

Below: The Short 'Folder' was a simple floatplane used by the British for naval reconnaissance. For take-off the aeroplane was 'unfolded' and lowered on to the water by crane before the engine was started.

approach. In less than three weeks, Garros became the world's first air ace by shooting down five aircraft. Then the engine of his aeroplane seized as a result of the stresses imposed by the occasional bullet strike on the propeller. Coming down behind the German lines, Garros failed to destroy his aeroplane. It was seized with great interest by the Germans.

Above: This cutaway of an Albatros D Va fighter reveals the type of construction used in many German fighters during the closing stages of World War I.

The Germans, too, had been working on an interrupter gear, but the capture of the Garros's Type L added great impetus. In just a few days the design team working for the Germans' Dutch manufacturer Fokker came up with a fully practical interrupter gear that was tried on a Fokker M.5k monoplane. These tests were wholly successful and the combination of M.5k and interrupted gun was put in production as the E I, the world's first true fighter. Production was fairly slow, so the impact of the new weapon was only slowly recognized by the Allies. Variants up to the E IV were

Top: The Nieuport 17 was a classic French fighter, combining adequate firepower with good performance and great agility.

Above: The Albatros D V was an effort to match the latest Allied fighters by refining an existing concept and adding more power. A worthwhile warplane but was kept in service too long. The lower wing also displayed a tendency to break away.

produced, and German aces such as Oswald Boelcke and Max Immelmann rose to prominence on the type.

In fact this 'Eindecker' – monoplane – was an indifferent performer in most respects, only its armament making possible the 'Fokker Scourge' of the period from autumn 1915 to spring 1916, when the Allies responded with their own but vastly superior biplane fighters. The Allies still lacked an effective interrupter gear, so the British Airco D.H.2 was a pusher – with a rear-mounted propeller – to leave the nose free, while the French Nieuport 11 had its gun above the upper wing to fire from the propeller disc. These two aircraft swept the Fokkers from the sky, and in the process opened a see-saw technical battle – that has continued to the present – with each side striving to produce a better machine than the other.

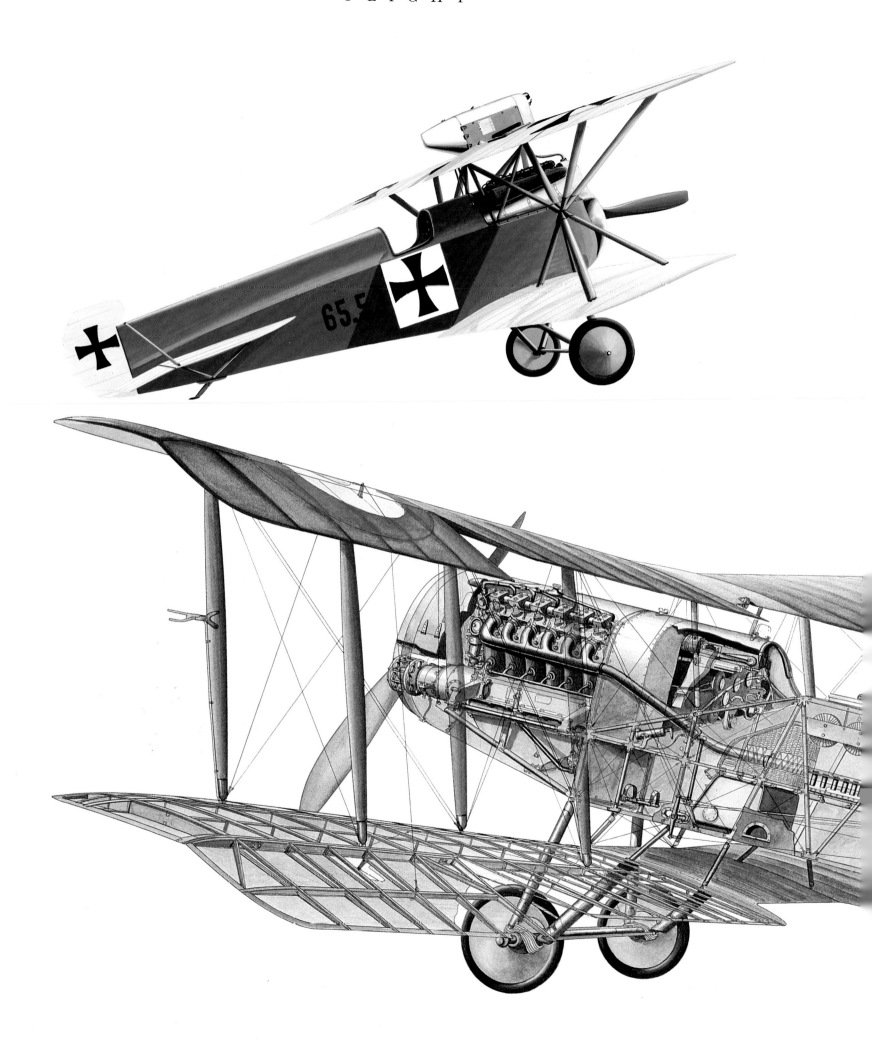

The Germans responded to this challenge with a number of types, of which the most significant were the Albatros fighters (successively improved D I, D II, D III and D V biplanes), the Fokker fighters (Dr I triplane, D VII biplane and D VIII parasol monoplane) and the Pfalz D III biplane. The Allies had meanwhile perfected an interrupter gear and countered, over the last two years of the war, with the Royal Aircraft Factory S.E.5/5a and the Sopwith Pup, Triplane and Camel in British service, and the Nieuport 17 and the SPAD S.7 and S.13 in French service.

These were agile machines generally of high performance and fitted with a single or, later, twin interrupted guns. As such they were the ultimate arbiters of the air war, for though their prey was often other fighters, their main task was in destroying the enemy's two-seaters, the aircraft that could damage the ground forces on whom the war was thought to hinge. The two-seaters themselves underwent enormous development along lines parallel to those of the fighters. Early two-seaters were mostly of the inherently stable type that was thought best-suited to reconnaissance. But these could not be effectively manoeuvred and fell easy prey to agile fighters. So obsolescent planes like the Royal Aircraft Factory B.E.2, the German Aviatik B/C-series and the French Blériots and Caudrons were gradually replaced by less stable machines of higher

Left: Known as the 'Star-strutter' because of its unusual interplane bracing, the Hansa-Brandenburg D I single-seat fighter was designed in Germany but built in Austria-Hungary during 1916 and 1917.

Below: The Bristol F.2B was the finest two-seat fighter of World War I through its combination of high performance, considerable agility, great strength and good firepower, the last including the 'rear stinger' operated by the gunner.

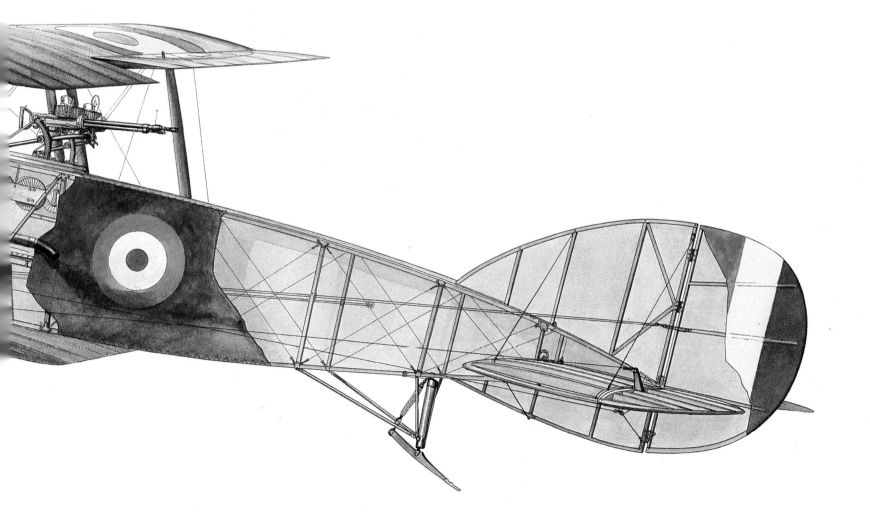

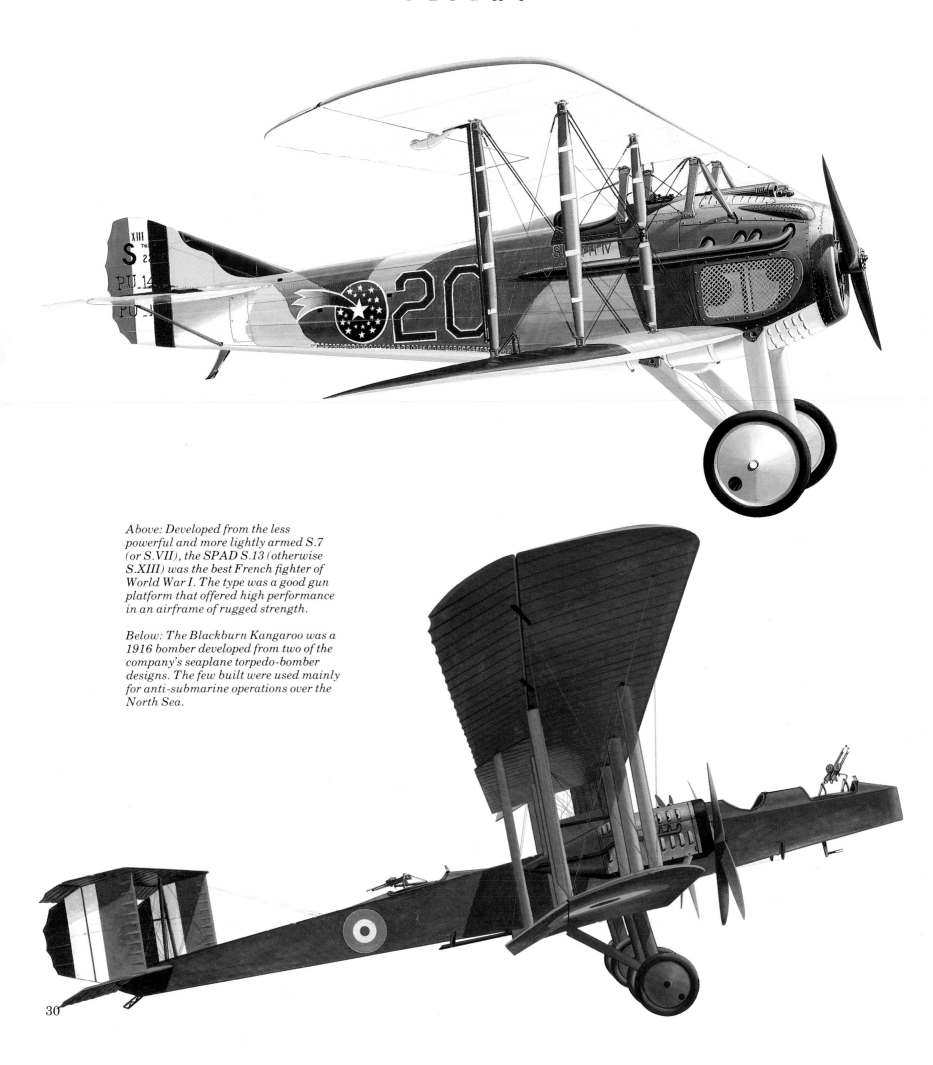

Above: Developed from the less powerful and more lightly armed S.7 (or S.VII), the SPAD S.13 (otherwise S.XIII) was the best French fighter of World War I. The type was a good gun platform that offered high performance in an airframe of rugged strength.

Below: The Blackburn Kangaroo was a 1916 bomber developed from two of the company's seaplane torpedo-bomber designs. The few built were used mainly for anti-submarine operations over the North Sea.

Left: With the similar G V, the Gotha G IV was Germany's best short-range heavy bomber of World War I.

Below: The Airco (de Havilland) D.H.4 was a high-performance day bomber whose sole (but major) tactical failing was the location of the vulnerable main fuel tank between the pilot and the gunner, who found it difficult to communicate.

performance. Some were indifferent machines – like the Royal Aircraft Factory R.E.8. Nonetheless they were built in substantial numbers. Others were first-class combat machines well able to handle fighters when properly flown so that the pilot could use his fixed gun when the observer/gunner could not bring his trainable weapon to bear. Classics of this genre were the Breguet Bre.14, the DFW C-series, the Halberstadt C V, the LFG (Roland) C II, the LVG C V and VI, the Rumpler C-series and the Salmson 2.

It also became necessary to escort reconnaissance and artillery observation two-seaters. This led to the development of potent two-seater

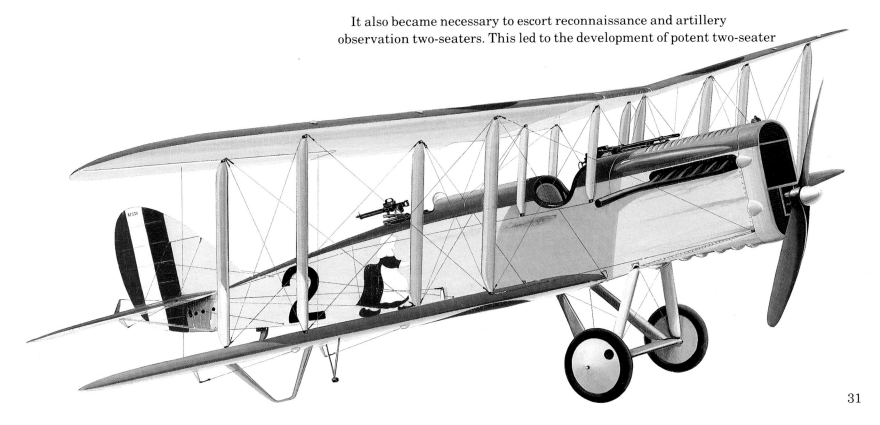

fighters – the classic example is the Bristol F.2B Fighter that remained in service until the late 1920s. The Germans also developed a similar type, though in this instance a light C-type with a secondary ground-attack role. The best of these were the Halberstadt CL II and IV, and the Hannover CL II and IIIa.

Inevitably any spot worth photographing may be worth bombing and it was not long before the first primitive bombs were being dropped onto enemy positions. Often these were light bombs released from *ad hoc* mountings on single- and two-seaters, but as the war developed the need emerged for specialist aircraft able to carry an effective bombload and defensive armament in a sturdy airframe. In this field the Germans led the way from 1916 with the Friedrichshafen and Gotha G-series bombers. These were large twin-engined pusher biplanes. The Allies preferred single-engined aircraft carrying a smaller bombload at higher speed for tactical rather than operational attacks. The French mainstay was the Bre.14 that also served in the reconnaissance role, while the British used the Airco (de Havilland) D.H.4 and D.H.9 aircraft, the latter locating the two crew members close together to overcome the D.H.4's main tactical failing which was siting a fuel tank between the two airmen. Production of these Allied bombers far outstripped German G-series production and in the last year of the war they attained very useful results.

The German two-seaters, especially those of the CL-series, could often carry bombs for the light attack role, and the British often used their fighters for close support of the ground forces with machine-gun fire and light bombs carried on racks under the wings or under the fuselage. The concept was taken to its extreme in the Sopwith Salamander, a so-called trench fighter derived from the Snipe fighter with extensive armour

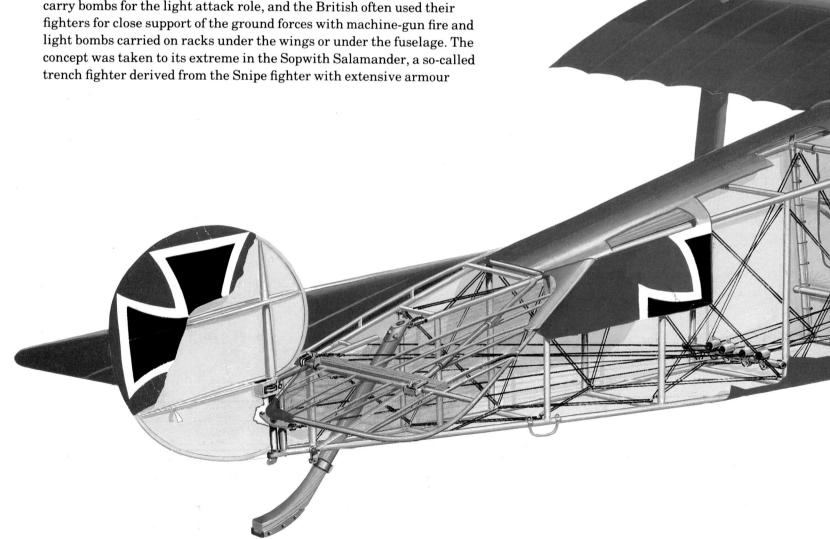

The Fokker Dr I was designed in direct response to the Sopwith Triplane. It was superbly manoeuvrable but had indifferent performance, suiting it for defensive operations by high-quality pilots only. This cutaway reveals the construction favoured by designer Reinhold Platz, with a welded steel-tube fuselage covered with aluminium and fabric skinning, and basically cantilever wings of deep-section wooden construction covered with plywood and fabric.

protection and great ammunition capacity for its twin guns. It was also tried with multi-gun batteries aligned to fire obliquely forward and downward. As the war began to turn against them in 1917, the Germans sought to redress some of the balance with specialist close support aircraft such as the Junkers CL I and J I. Both of these were of all-metal construction but the former a low-wing monoplane while the latter was a massive sesquiplane. It had one and a half wings – the 'half' mounted below the massive main wing. With the exception of the J I, none of these specialist close-support aircraft was built in large numbers as the war ended shortly after they had been developed.

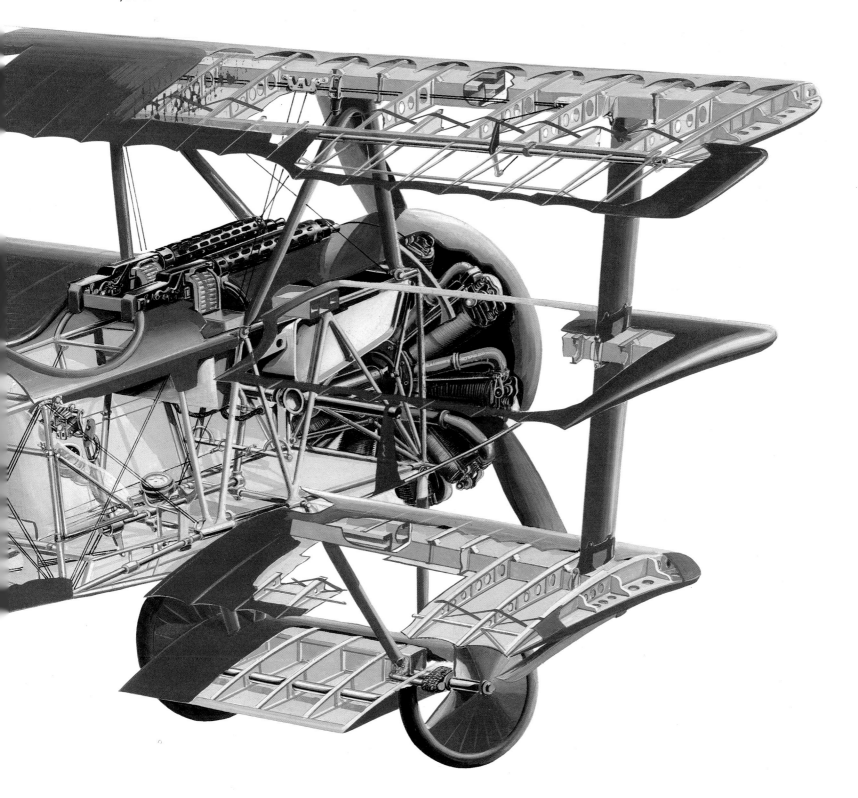

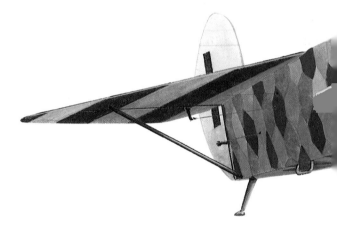

All the major powers attempted strategic bombing in World War I. The British began with raids by naval aircraft on German Zeppelin airship facilities, but the heavy bomber war then expanded. The British built the Handley Page O/100 and O/400 twin-engined bombers, and nearly got the massive Handley Page V/1500 four-engined bomber operational. The Germans flew their Gothas – which were supplemented and then supplanted by airships – against targets in the UK and their R-series giant bombers against a variety of long-range targets. The Russians operated their Sikorsky Ilya Muromets four-engined bombers against Austro-Hungarian and German targets. And the Italians built the extraordinary series of Caproni bombers which were also used by the Americans and the French. The Germans also had some fascinating giant bombers nearing operational capability as the war ended. Along with the V/1500, these might have opened a period of true strategic bombing.

Left: The LFG (Roland) C II was an excellent reconnaissance and escort aeroplane whose deep fuselage resulted in the nickname Walfisch (whale).

Below: Though only two reached the Western Front before the end of World War I, the Packard-Le Pére LUSAC II was the finest aeroplane designed specifically for the US air arm in that war. The type was a two-seat fighter.

Above: Platz's last fighter of World War I was the superb Fokker D VIII using the same type of basic structure as the Dr I but with a parasol monoplane wing of the cantilever type. The D VIII was too late to see widespread service.

Naval aviation was also significant in World War I. The main weight of development and production was devoted to flying boats intended for maritime reconnaissance and, as the war progressed, anti-submarine patrol. The finest of these were the British boats, stemming from the efforts of Commander John Porte at the Seaplane Experimental Establishment at Felixstowe, and the American boats developed by Glenn Curtiss. Several other nations also developed floatplane and even flying boat fighters. The most important of these being the Macchi series in Italy and the Hansa-Brandenburg series used by Austria-Hungary and Germany. The arena in which the floatplane – that is an seaplane with floats instead of a hull – found its greatest role, however, was torpedo attack. Here the British led the way with classics such as the Short 184 and Sopwith Cuckoo. World War I also witnessed the birth of the aircraft-carrier under British leadership. By the end of the war the Royal Navy had two aircraft-carriers in commission, with several important combat aircraft under development, replacements for World War I's simple conversions of standard landplanes.

Previous page: A type that still commands enormous affection, the Sopwith Pup was a supremely agile and tractable fighter armed with only one synchronized machine-gun.

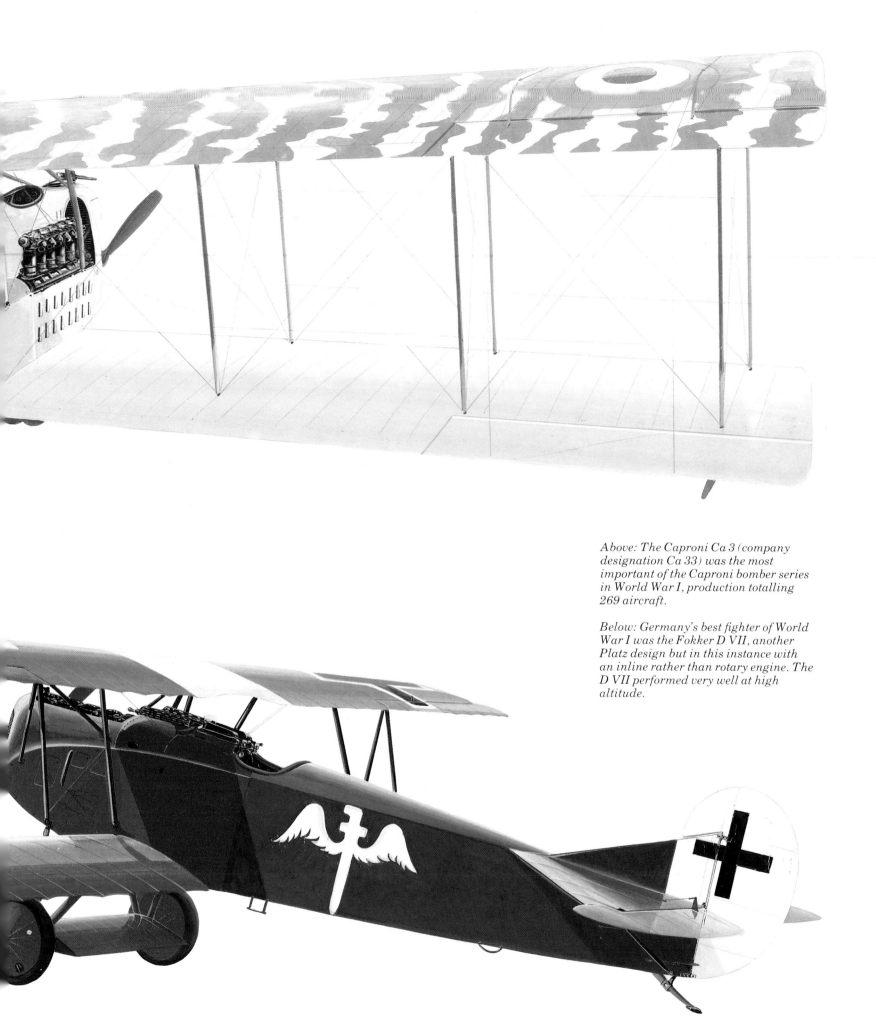

Above: The Caproni Ca 3 (company designation Ca 33) was the most important of the Caproni bomber series in World War I, production totalling 269 aircraft.

Below: Germany's best fighter of World War I was the Fokker D VII, another Platz design but in this instance with an inline rather than rotary engine. The D VII performed very well at high altitude.

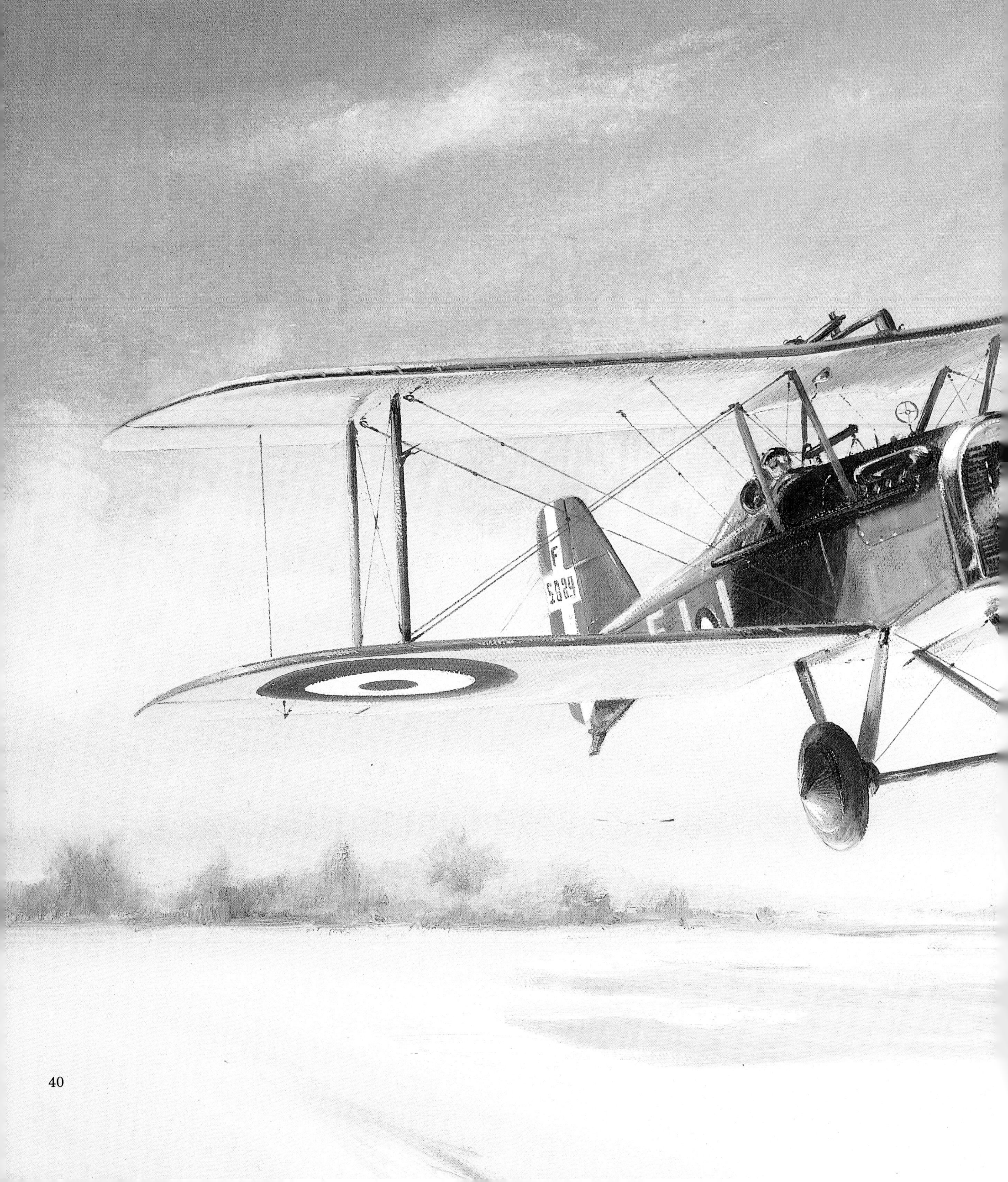

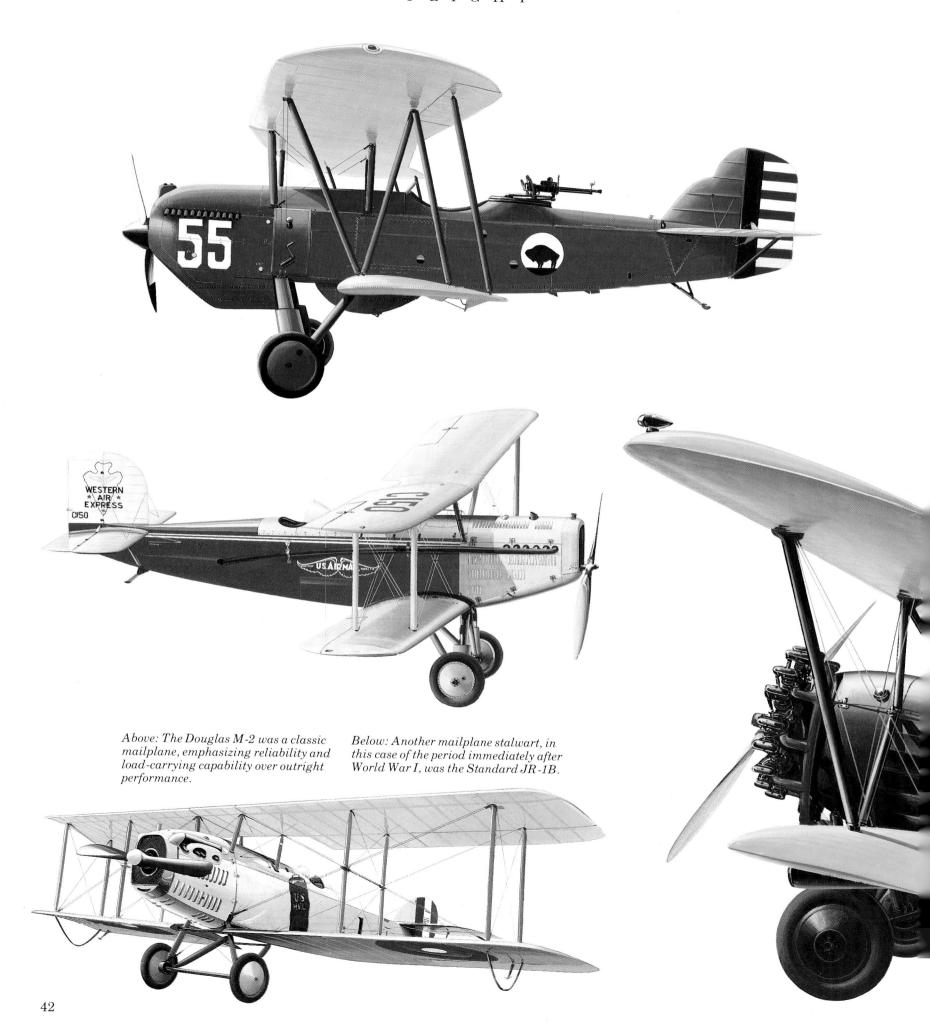

Above: The Douglas M-2 was a classic mailplane, emphasizing reliability and load-carrying capability over outright performance.

Below: Another mailplane stalwart, in this case of the period immediately after World War I, was the Standard JR-1B.

CHAPTER FOUR: THE MODERN AEROPLANE

Left: The Curtiss O-1 Falcon was the US Army Air Corps' main reconnaissance aeroplane in the late 1920s and early 1930s.

Below: The Pitcairn Super Mailwing was used from 1928 by a number of air-mail carriers, and is seen here in the livery of Eastern Air Transport, precursor of the present Eastern Air Lines.

Pages 40–1: With the Sopwith Camel the mainstay of the British fighter arm in the closing stages of World War I, the Royal Aircraft Factory S.E.5a was strong and fast, and though not as agile as the Camel it was a superior gun platform.

World War I had been a watershed in the development of aviation. In 1914 the aeroplane was little more than a curiosity of only marginal practical value. By 1918 it was a thoroughly practical machine in its many forms capable of undertaking with great success a vast array of tasks. Four years of war had forced the technological pace at an unprecedented rate, and the aeroplane was structurally sounder and aerodynamically more advanced to make effective use of the increasingly powerful and reliable engines now available.

The development of the engine was as responsible as any other single factor for the emergence of the aeroplane as a working machine during World War I. At the beginning of the war, there were few engines that could develop more than 100 hp and these were often temperamental units of poor reliability. The classic rotary engine, for example, could not be throttled in the conventional sense. It had to be controlled by cutting the ignition to a selected number of cylinders, causing in these cylinders a build-up of fuel that would explode when the ignition was restored! By 1918 engines of 400 hp were becoming common. Though the rotary still had its adherents for fighters, the big water-cooled inline and new air-cooled radial engines offered greater development potential as well as considerably improved reliability. Yet the availability of this additional

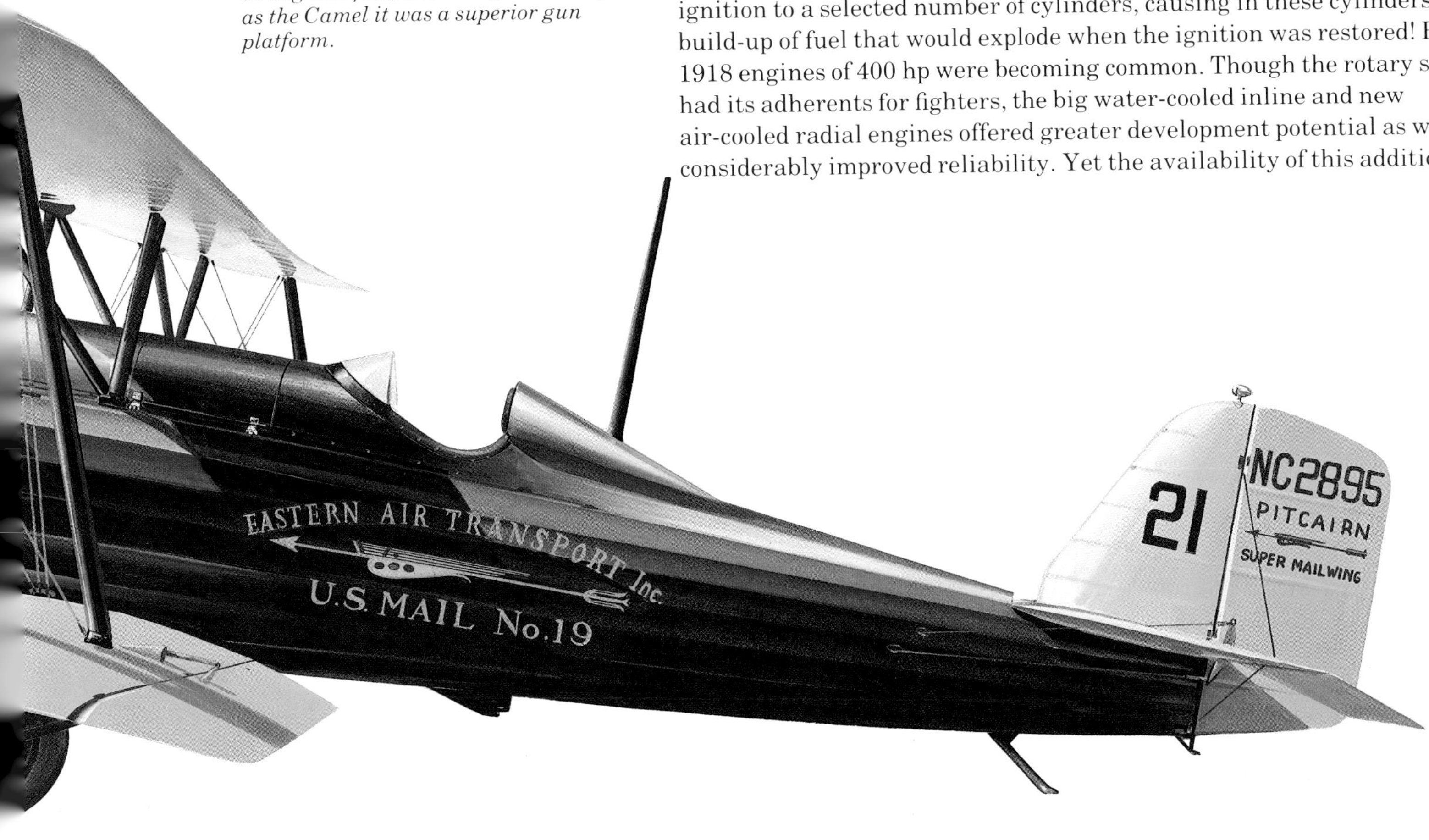

The Stearman Speedmail operated by Varney Air Lines in the air-mail role was powered by a 525-hp Pratt & Whitney Hornet radial in a neat nose installation for a speed of 126 mph and a range of 780 miles.

horsepower had transformed the aeroplane not so much in outright flight performance, where maximum speeds had increased from about 100 mph to only about 140 mph, but rather in payload. The 'heavy-lift' service aircraft of 1914 were hard-pressed to carry more than 300 lb of disposable load, yet some of 1918's aircraft could carry several thousand pounds: the Zeppelin-Staaken R VI could carry 4,405 lb of bombs and the Handley Page V/1500 7,500 lb. These loads could, of course, be carried only over short ranges, but with reduced bombloads such aircraft had impressive range.

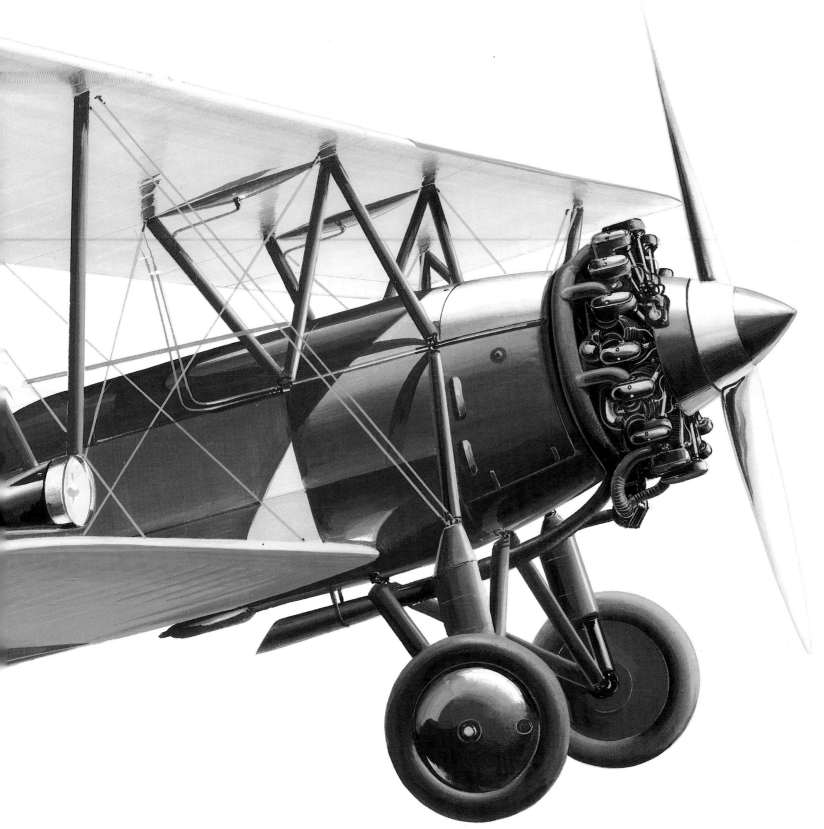

It was with considerable technical maturity that aircraft entered into the period of peace after World War I. But World War I was considered 'the war to end all wars' and with the onset of peace there was a severe curtailment in military spending. Air forces were compelled to make do with the aircraft that had been in production at the war's end and were cut back drastically in size. The public saw no reason for large armed services after the 'war to end all wars' and governments were all too willing to go along with the public sentiment for the simple reason that, with the single exception of the USA, the combatants had been virtually bankrupted by the war. The inevitable result was the loss of impetus in aeronautical development until the mid-1920s. The governments of the western nations were aware that the Great War had not been really the 'war to end all wars', but they were content to live with small, cheap forces, confident that there would be sufficient warning of impending hostilities to allow re-equipment and expansion of their forces.

The air forces of the early 1920s were equipped largely with obsolescent World War I aircraft. Even when these had to be replaced their successors adhered to the same basic design philosophy. Improvements were made, but these were of a relatively minor nature: radio equipment, better instrumentation and oxygen for high-altitude flight. The primary structure was now of metal, but was done to increase aircraft's service lives

and reduce reliance on the imported wood that had come to be in very short supply during World War I. The structure remained essentially unaltered, with metal substituted for wood. A doped fabric covering was still standard.

Fighters are generally considered the cutting edge of aeronautical technology – and it was a comparatively poor state if you looked at the fighters fielded by the UK and USA during the 1920s. The British Armstrong Whitworth Siskin, Gloster Gamecock and Grebe, and Bristol Bulldog and the American Boeing FB/P-12 and Curtiss FC/P-1/P-6 series all adhered to the World War I philosophy of a biplane layout with fixed tailwheel landing gear and an armament of two fixed machine guns located with their breeches within reach of the pilot so that he could clear any jams. The other aeronautical power of the period was France, which followed much the same pattern as the UK, albeit with some modification to allow the introduction of better streamlining and on occasion a monoplane layout. It is worth noting, however, that the USSR was making great efforts to develop an indigenous aircraft industry and, with assistance from Germany, moved rapidly towards the forefront of aeronautical technology. This fact was not appreciated outside the USSR

Top: Powered by three 20-hp Wright
J-5 radials, the Keystone Pathfinder
was an indifferent performer and built
in only small numbers.

Far left: During the 1920s there was
considerable enthusiasm for the added
lift of bracing struts faired into aerofoil
contours, as on this Wright-Bellanca
W.B.2 'Columbia' long-range
aeroplane. The type was pipped to the
New York-Paris prize by Lindbergh's
Ryan NYP, but was then flown by
Clarence Chamberlin to a world
distance record of 3,911 miles from New
York to Eisleben in Germany.

Left: The Sikorsky S-35 was an
unsuccessful contender for the New
York to Paris flight achieved so
brilliantly by Charles Lindbergh in
May 1927.

47

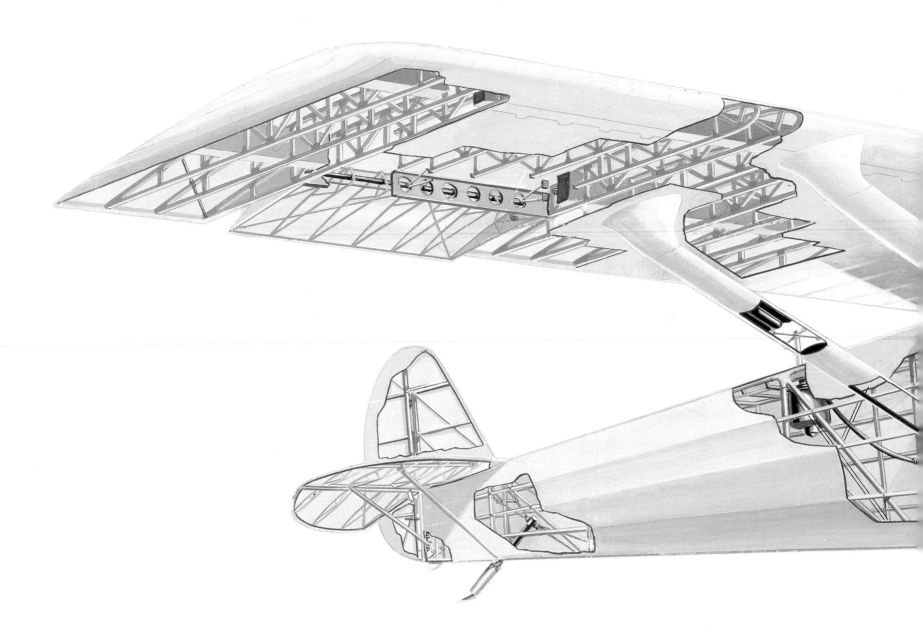

at the time, but a number of advanced aircraft were developed and placed in production for the fledgling Soviet fighter arm.

The same basic pattern can be discerned in the development of bombers, where ex-World War I aircraft and their conceptual descendants were the norm until the late 1920s and early 1930s. The sole exception was again the USSR where an ambitious policy of local development produced excellent aircraft that often featured the best of foreign ideas and items, when the latter could be imported for short-term expediency and then copied and developed for long-term utility.

All this is not to say that there were no technical developments in the period, but that these developments only found their way in service aircraft on a piecemeal and very slow basis. There had been all-metal aircraft before World War I – the unsuccessful Levavasseur-designed Antoinette Monobloc – and during World War I – the Dornier and Junkers aircraft. But it was 1920 before the forward-looking Short Silver Streak appeared with an all-metal structure that included a metal *semi-*

The Ryan NYP was built specifically for Charles Lindbergh's solo flight from New York to Paris in May 1927, and though a conventional aeroplane in most respects had the unusual feature of forward vision by periscope as the fuel tank occupied the complete depth of the fuselage forward of the cockpit.

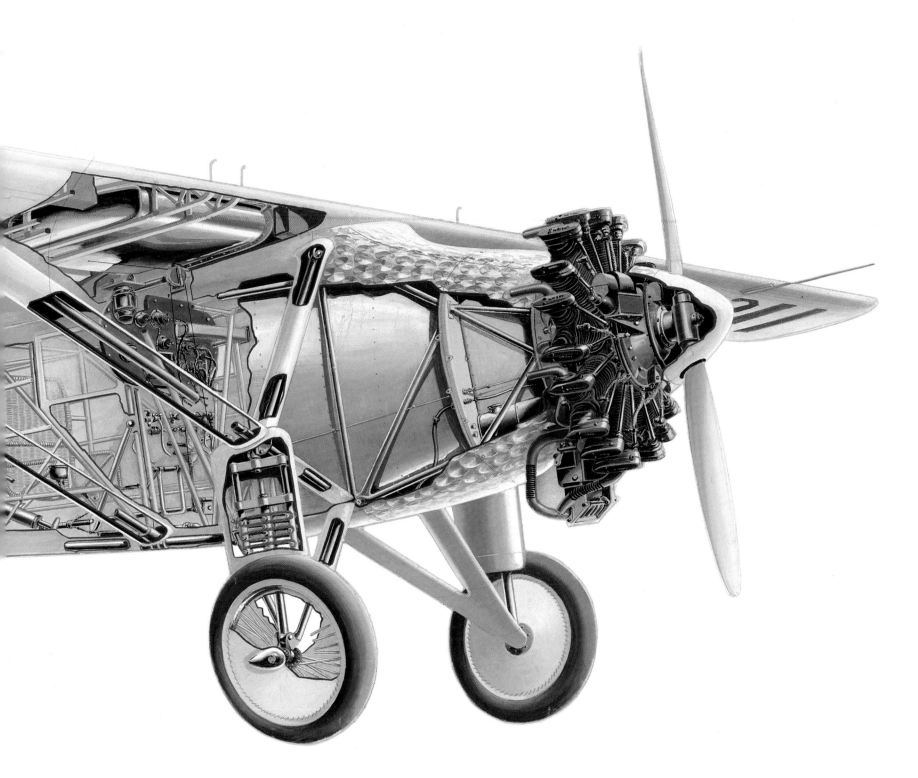

monocoque (stressed-skin) fuselage. Even farther-sighted in its own way was the stressed-skin metal wing developed by Dr Adolph Rohrbach in Germany and later in the USA during the first half of the 1920s. Rohrbach realized how high in drag the Junkers type of wing with its streamwise corrugated skinning was in comparison, for example, with the smooth-surfaced cantilever wings of wooden construction developed for Fokker aircraft by Reinhold Platz during 1917. In 1919 Rohrbach combined the concepts to produce the world's first stressed-skin wing, initially of the semi-cantilever type with bracing struts and/or wires, but later of the fully cantilever type with the skinning taking much of the aerodynamic and structural load supported by the wings.

Previous page: The Avro 504 was first flown in 1913, was used for military and training purposes in World War I, and then remained in service as a military and civil trainer right through the 1920s.

Right: The Ford Tri-Motor is a classic aeroplane of its period, a ruthlessly reliable and robust type of all-metal construction at a time when most civil aircraft were fabric-skinned. This example of the 4-AT series was built in March 1928 and used in Commander Richard E. Byrd's Antarctic expedition.

Below: Another Antarctic pioneer was this Fokker F.VIIA-3m. The type became a great airliner of the period between the World Wars in both its short-wing F.VIIA and long-wing F.VIIB versions.

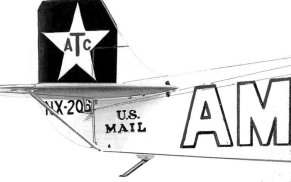

Another far-sighted technical development of the early 1920s was retractable landing gear. Designers had for some time been considering the use of such landing gear as a means of reducing drag and enhancing performance but were deterred not so much by the mechanical complexity of such gear as by its weight. Many designers thought – probably correctly in the 1920s – that the additional weight would erode most of the anticipated performance gain. However, in 1920 the Wright R.B. high-wing monoplane racer was developed with retractable gear and, though the advantages of the system were evident, it was the 1930s before retractable landing gear began to appear on anything other than experimental or racing aircraft.

FLOYD BENNETT

ATC

ERICA Peace

Below: Fokker's American subsidiary was variously known as the Atlantic Aircraft Manufacturing Company, the Fokker Aircraft Corporation and, in partnership with General Motors, the General Aviation Corporation. This is an example of its products, a military C-2 modelled on the Dutch F.VIIA-3m and used unsuccessfully by Byrd for a transatlantic flight that ended in the sea just off the French coast during 1927.

53

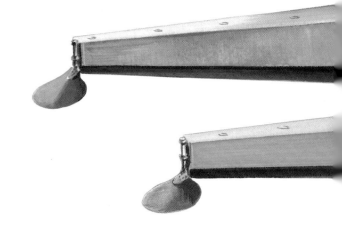

It should be noted here that two of the greatest spurs to technical development in the 1920s were racing and record breaking. Racing had been pioneered before World War I and reappeared in the 1920s. The two most notable competitions were the Pulitzer Trophy landplane races in the USA and the Schneider Trophy seaplane races held internationally. The Pulitzer races were instrumental in the development of high-output engines and advanced aerodynamics in the USA, while the more important Schneider races achieved even more in the same two fields on the international level. The three countries most heavily involved in the Schneider races were Italy, the UK and the USA. The aviation industries of all three countries benefited immeasurably from the series, which also generated enormous public enthusiasm and thus promoted overall awareness of and interest in aviation matters.

Record breaking also had its part to play in this process and in itself additionally spurred technical developments as men sought to fly faster, farther and higher. The aircraft produced specifically for record breaking were in a way anomalies as they were optimized for a small and very specialized role, but the dissemination of technical features from all three record-breaking fields into the body of aircraft design as a whole allowed the steady improvement of aircraft from about 1930 onwards. Such records were set mostly by military aircraft, or aircraft sponsored by the military in expectation of technical spin-offs that would improve service aircraft. However, there were a few purely civil record-breakers, including the legendary Howard Hughes, but the field in which civil aviation excelled was the long-distance flight either across the world with stops, or across oceans non-stop.

Such efforts began with the US Navy's first transatlantic flight in 1919 using Curtiss NC flying boats, the first non-stop flight across the Atlantic in a Vickers Vimy by Alcock and Brown, and the first aerial circumnavigation of the Earth by the Douglas World Cruisers of the US Army. Soon after World War I British fliers were launching themselves on

Previous page: The American equivalent of the Avro 504 was the Curtiss JN-4 'Jenny', which was used for training during World War I and then went on to build a huge reputation as a 'barnstorming' aeroplane in the 1920s and 1930s.

Above: Yet another aeroplane type used in the Byrd Antarctic expeditions was the Curtiss-Wright T-32 Condor II, which could be fitted with float or ski alighting gear. The type was developed in landplane form as an airliner, but was eclipsed in this role by the modern monoplanes just beginning to appear on the scene.

Right: This Lockheed Sirius was built for Charles Lindbergh in his capacity as route surveyor for Pan American, and in this float-equipped form was used in Lindbergh's 1930 route-proving operations in the north Pacific.

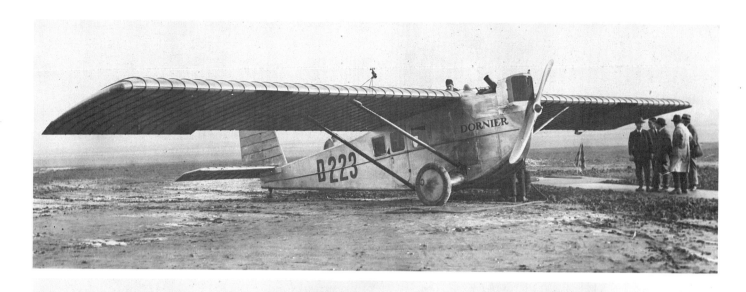

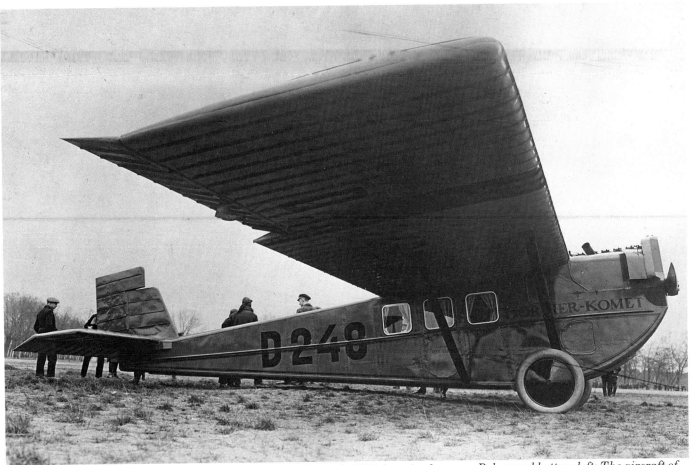

Left above: The Dornier Komet of the early 1920s was constructed of metal. Left centre: A Junkers G24 of the mid-1920s, was the first airliner with passenger seatbelts.

Above: On its early 1920s' service from Berlin to London via Amsterdam, the Dornier Komet I offered 'service as luxurious as an American parlor car'.

Below and bottom left: The aircraft of the early years were as potent an attraction as modern racing cars.

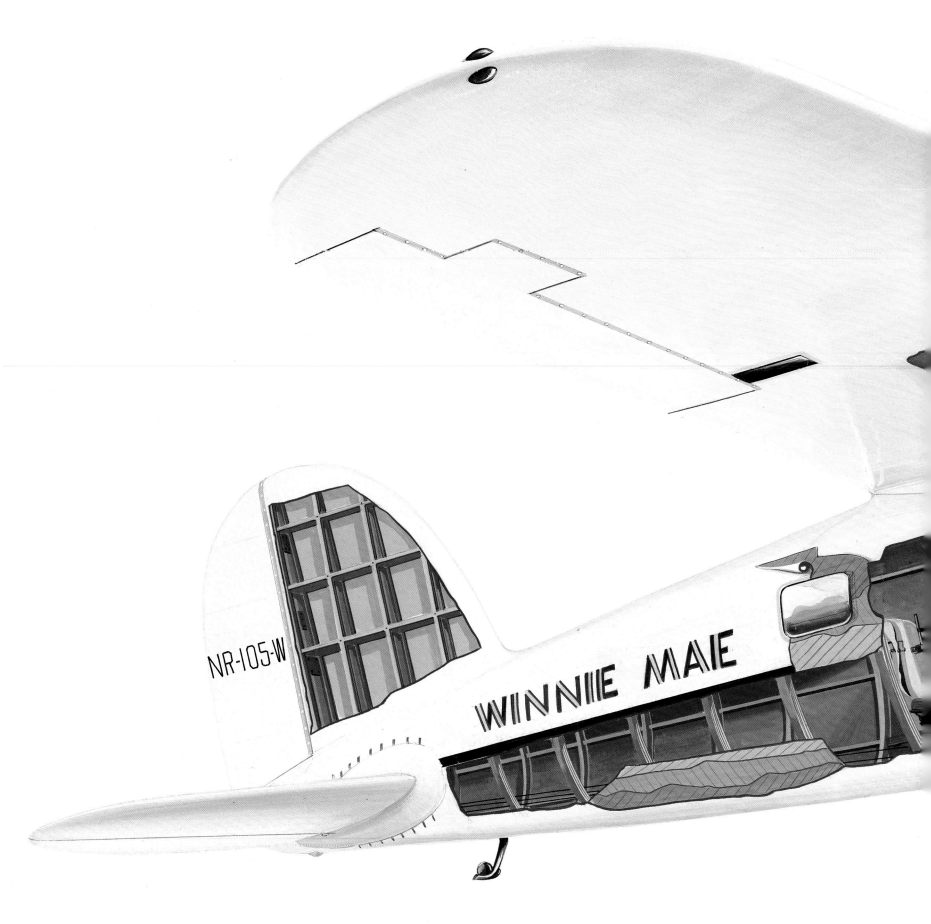

The Lockheed 5B Vega named Winnie Mae *was used by Wiley Post for the first solo flight round the world in July 1933, covering 15,596 miles in 7 days, 18 hours and 49 minutes. The aeroplane was also used for other celebrated flights in its basic two-seat form.*

flights to Australia and South Africa – stopping at points in between these imperial outposts – while the French flew to West Africa and then out across the South Atlantic to South America. Other world-spanning flights followed but the culmination of this great expansion of the air transport concept reached its peak with the first crossing of the Pacific from California to Australia by Charles Kingsford-Smith in a Fokker tri-motor in 1928. Less dramatic, but no less important in a number of ways, were flights across mountain ranges, deserts, the poles and other remote geographical and climatic regions.

But the most vital single exploit was the first solo non-stop crossing of the North Atlantic during May 1927 by Charles Lindbergh in a Ryan NYP single-engined monoplane. Lindbergh flew from New York to Paris, covering some 3,600 miles in 33 hours 39 minutes. It was a triumph that set the western world alight, but must be seen in the context of a host of other record flights by men and women such as Wiley Post, Amelia Earhart, Amy Johnson, Clive Pangborn and Jim Mollison, who all achieved prodigious long-distance flights in Avro, Bellanca, de Havilland, Lockheed and other light planes fitted with additional fuel capacity.

Right: During the 1920s there was enormous interest in non-stop flights across the Atlantic and the man who captured the greatest acclaim was Charles Lindbergh for his 1927 solo flight eastward from New York to Paris. The westward flight, against the prevailing winds, was an altogether more difficult prospect, demanding greater endurance from the men as well as the machines. This is a long-range biplane of the type used by three Frenchmen (Tarascon, Orteig and Coli) in their effort.

Below: The Boeing P-26A 'Peashooter' was an interim type between the biplane and monoplane fighter eras, for although it was laid out as a monoplane it had the fixed landing gear and wire-braced wings of the biplane fighter.

Air transport of the definitive pattern had started after World War I, initially in the form of air-mail and courier services operated by the air forces for government use in the hectic political climate immediately after the war. But several British, French and German companies had registered themselves as airlines during the war, and it was not many months after the end of hostilities before the first commercial transports were buzzing round the skies of Europe. These were all converted bombers, the pilot retaining the standard open cockpit but the small number of passengers being crammed into a small cabin created within the fuselage and fitted out with light-weight wicker seats and windows let into the sides of the fuselage. This form of travel was uncomfortable and expensive, but proved increasingly popular as wealthier people began to appreciate the value of the speed with which they could move around Europe. Larger cities and the main resorts soon developed airfields, and as the volume of air transport increased during the early part of the decade manufacturers began to produce specialized airliners offering better – and ultimately luxurious – levels of comfort. The most important aircraft companies in this process were Armstrong Whitworth, de Havilland and Handley Page in the UK, Farman in France, Junkers in Germany and Fokker in the Netherlands, each with its own distinctive line of development.

Gradually, the network of airline routes expanded from Europe and South America, where Germany was instrumental in establishing a number of important airlines, to the imperial possessions of the major colonial powers in Africa and the East. Increasingly long-ranged landplanes were complemented by flying boats for these imperial routes. The British, French, Italians and, ultimately, the Americans all produced classic types that offered a combination of excellent accommodation for a small number of passengers, modest performance and great safety and reliability.

American air transport was limited through much of the 1920s to air mail, but once passengers were permitted US air transport took off with a vengeance. The routes had been proved in air mail operations, so the burgeoning air transport industry rapidly commissioned special versions of the larger mailplanes and then custom-designed airliners. But the real breakthrough came with Boeing's adoption of retractable landing gear and

Above: Another Lockheed Vega used for a classic flight was this Model 1 Vega used by Wilkins and Eielson for the first flight across the Arctic Ocean, and then for the first exploratory flight of Antarctica.

Left: Airliners under construction at the Fokker works in the 1920s.

Below left: Luxury was the order of the day for air travellers in the 1920s.

Above: The Potez 25 was produced in many variants during the 1920s for military, record-breaking and civil use, this being a military observation variant used as a mailplane.

Right: The opening of airline operations by machines such as these adapted Handley Page bombers was always an opportunity for pomp.

Below: The Junkers W 34 was a classic utility transport, and could operate on wheel, ski or float alighting gear.

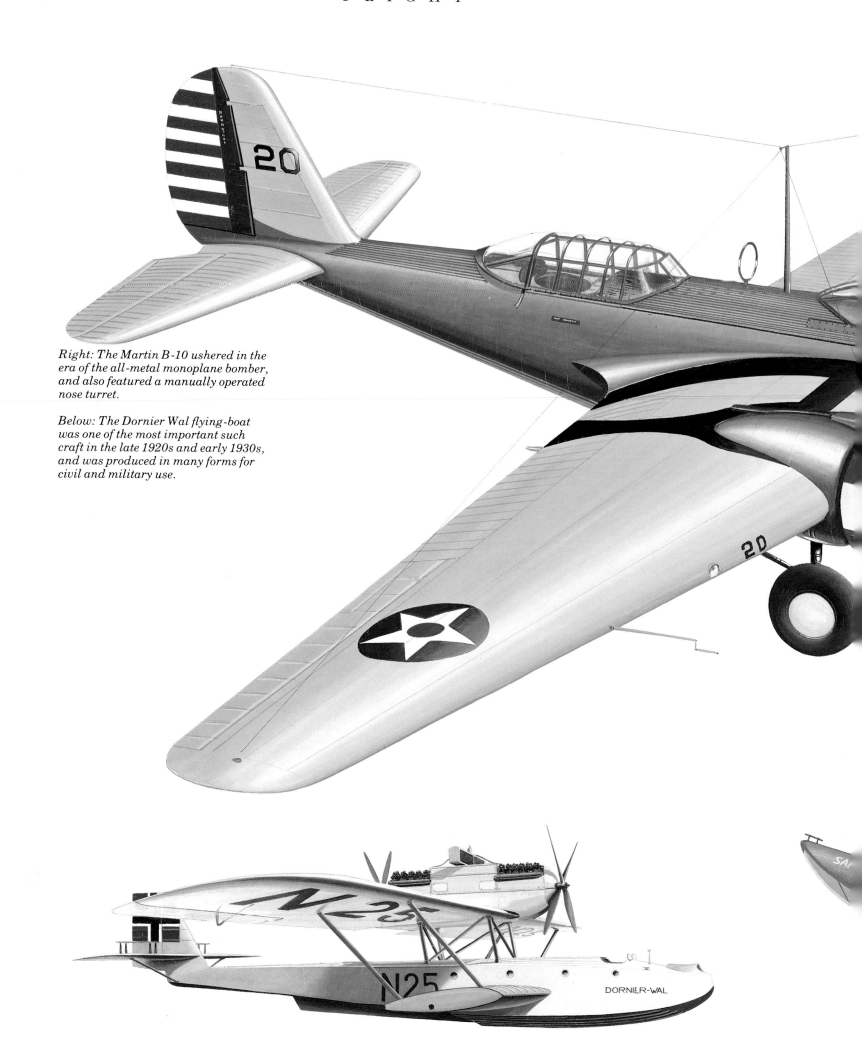

Right: The Martin B-10 ushered in the era of the all-metal monoplane bomber, and also featured a manually operated nose turret.

Below: The Dornier Wal flying-boat was one of the most important such craft in the late 1920s and early 1930s, and was produced in many forms for civil and military use.

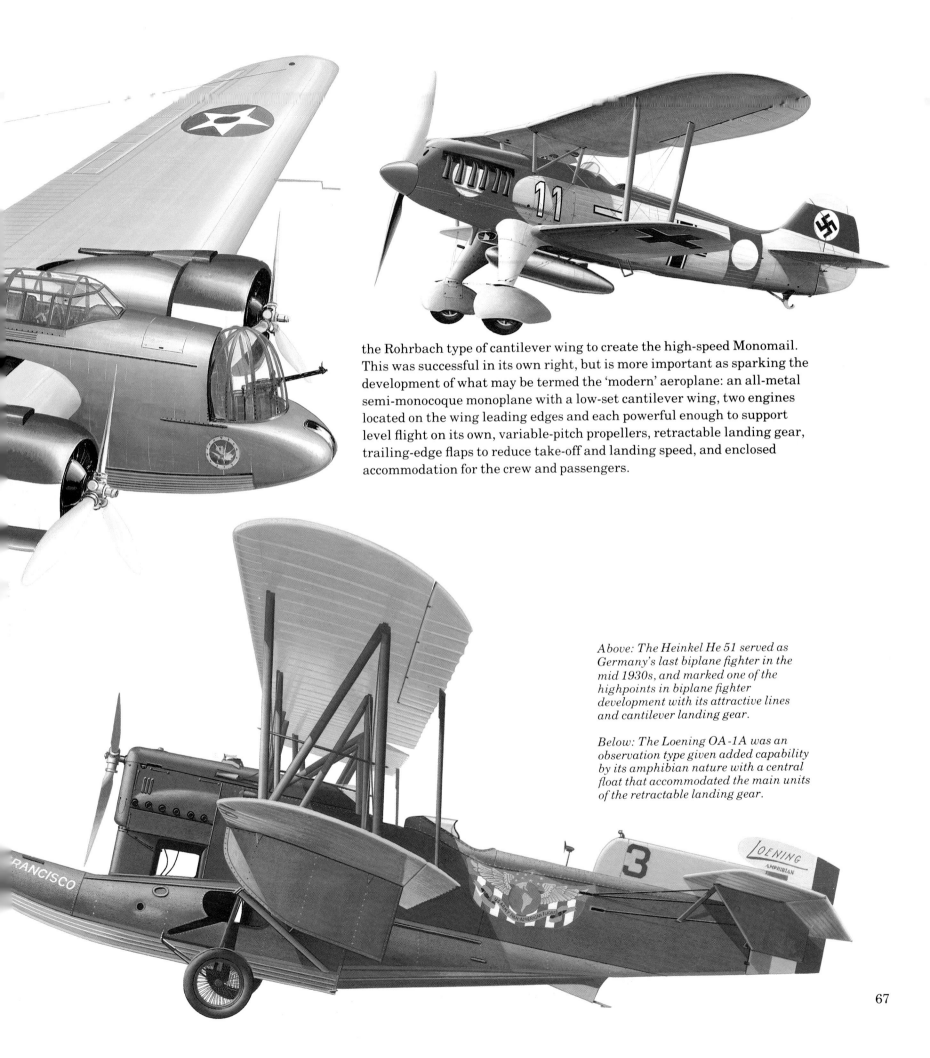

the Rohrbach type of cantilever wing to create the high-speed Monomail. This was successful in its own right, but is more important as sparking the development of what may be termed the 'modern' aeroplane: an all-metal semi-monocoque monoplane with a low-set cantilever wing, two engines located on the wing leading edges and each powerful enough to support level flight on its own, variable-pitch propellers, retractable landing gear, trailing-edge flaps to reduce take-off and landing speed, and enclosed accommodation for the crew and passengers.

Above: The Heinkel He 51 served as Germany's last biplane fighter in the mid 1930s, and marked one of the highpoints in biplane fighter development with its attractive lines and cantilever landing gear.

Below: The Loening OA-1A was an observation type given added capability by its amphibian nature with a central float that accommodated the main units of the retractable landing gear.

Right: A monster of its time, the Tupolev ANT-20 of the mid 1930s was a flying propaganda establishment complete with a film projector and processing laboratory, 'voice from the sky' loudspeaker system, pharmacy, printing press and leaflet dispenser.

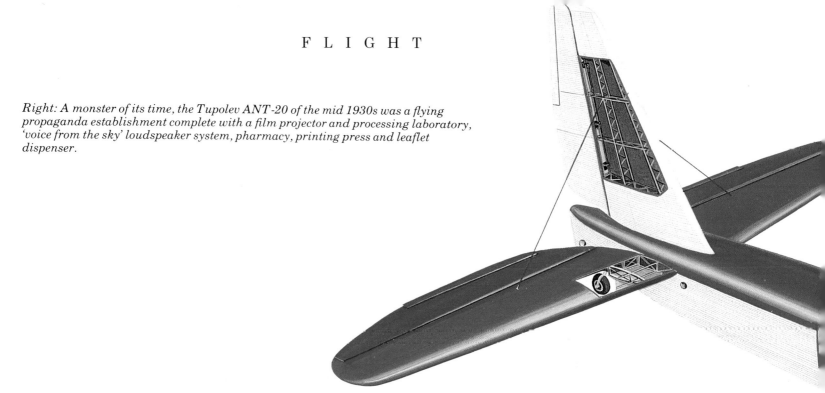

Above and below: Another extraordinary machine of the period was the Dornier Do X flying-boat, a scarcely practical machine intended as an airliner and powered by no fewer than 12 engines.

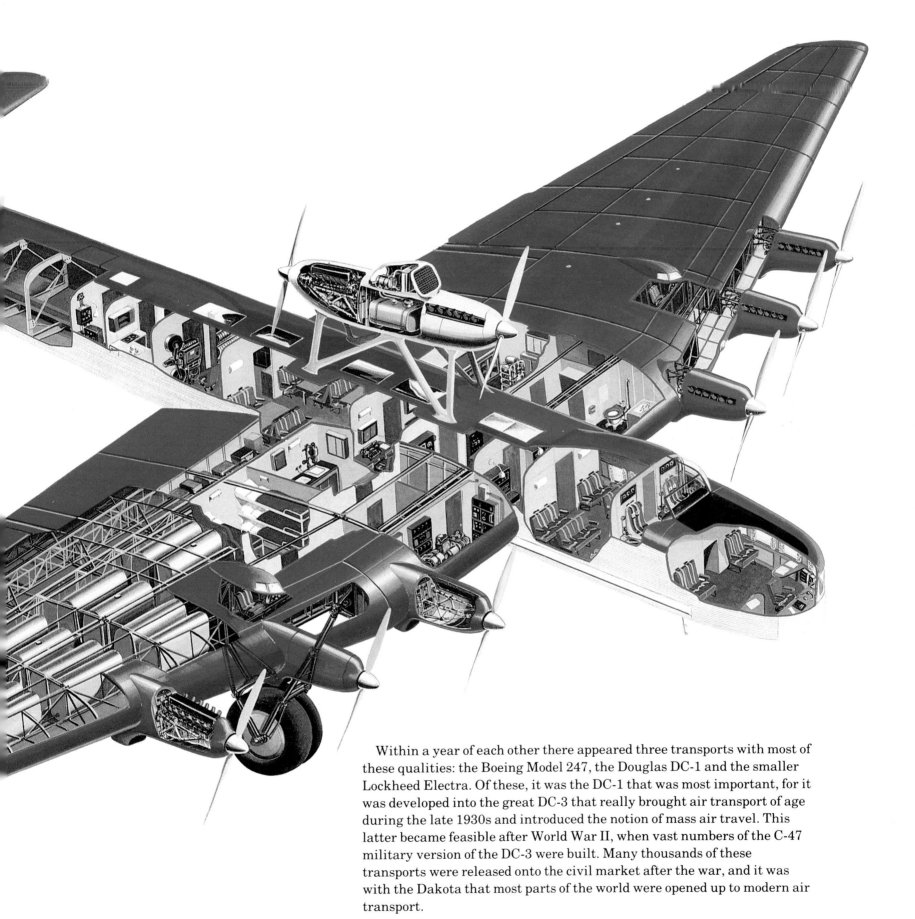

Within a year of each other there appeared three transports with most of these qualities: the Boeing Model 247, the Douglas DC-1 and the smaller Lockheed Electra. Of these, it was the DC-1 that was most important, for it was developed into the great DC-3 that really brought air transport of age during the late 1930s and introduced the notion of mass air travel. This latter became feasible after World War II, when vast numbers of the C-47 military version of the DC-3 were built. Many thousands of these transports were released onto the civil market after the war, and it was with the Dakota that most parts of the world were opened up to modern air transport.

Where the modern transport aircraft led in the mid-1930s the bomber followed, and soon all modern air forces were developing or introducing twin-engined bombers that incorporated all the best features of the modern transport as well as gun positions (soon supplemented and then

69

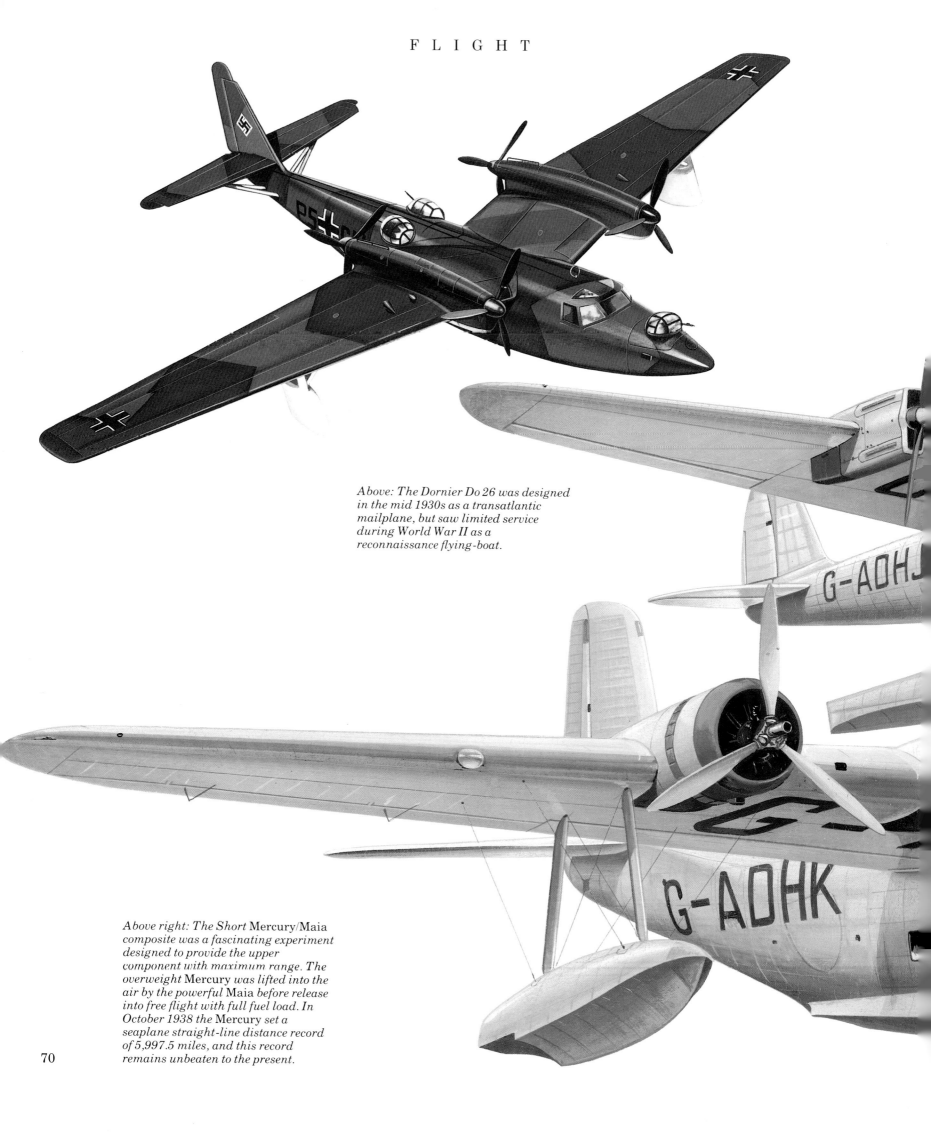

Above: The Dornier Do 26 was designed in the mid 1930s as a transatlantic mailplane, but saw limited service during World War II as a reconnaissance flying-boat.

Above right: The Short Mercury/Maia composite was a fascinating experiment designed to provide the upper component with maximum range. The overweight Mercury was lifted into the air by the powerful Maia before release into free flight with full fuel load. In October 1938 the Mercury set a seaplane straight-line distance record of 5,997.5 miles, and this record remains unbeaten to the present.

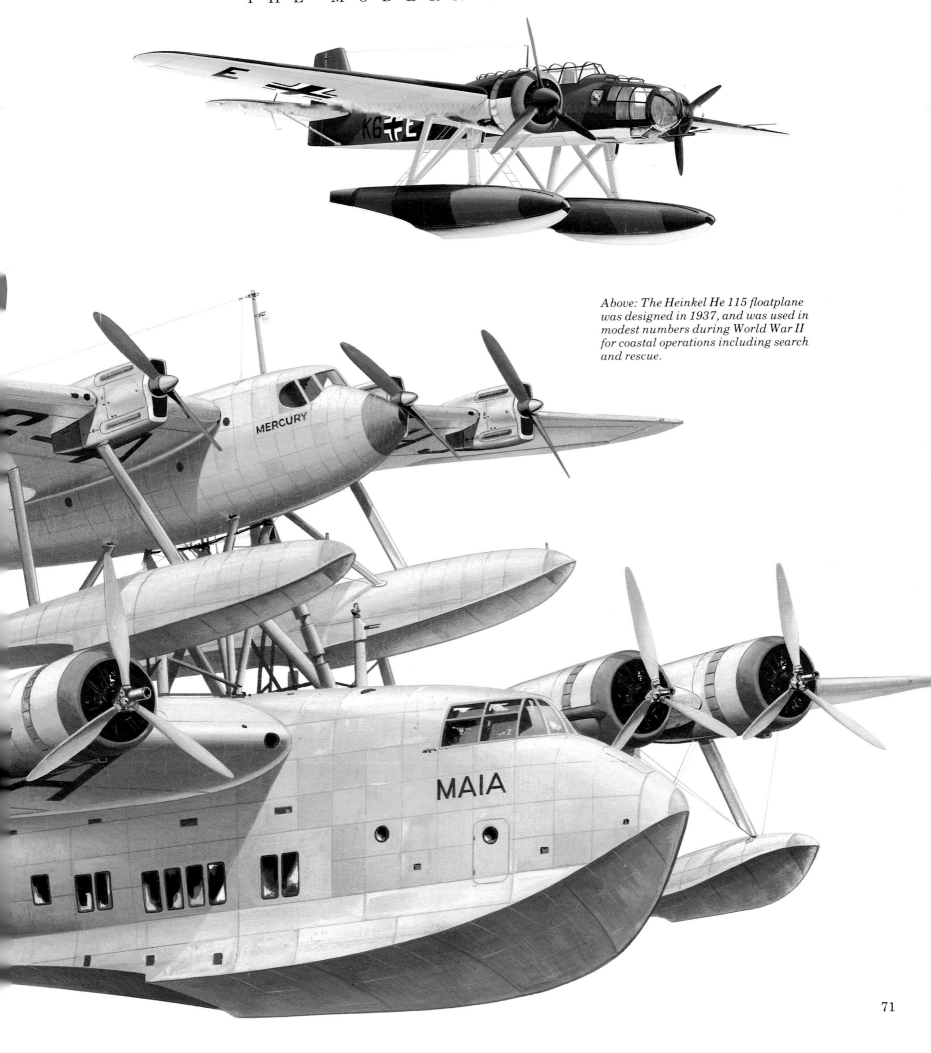

Above: The Heinkel He 115 floatplane was designed in 1937, and was used in modest numbers during World War II for coastal operations including search and rescue.

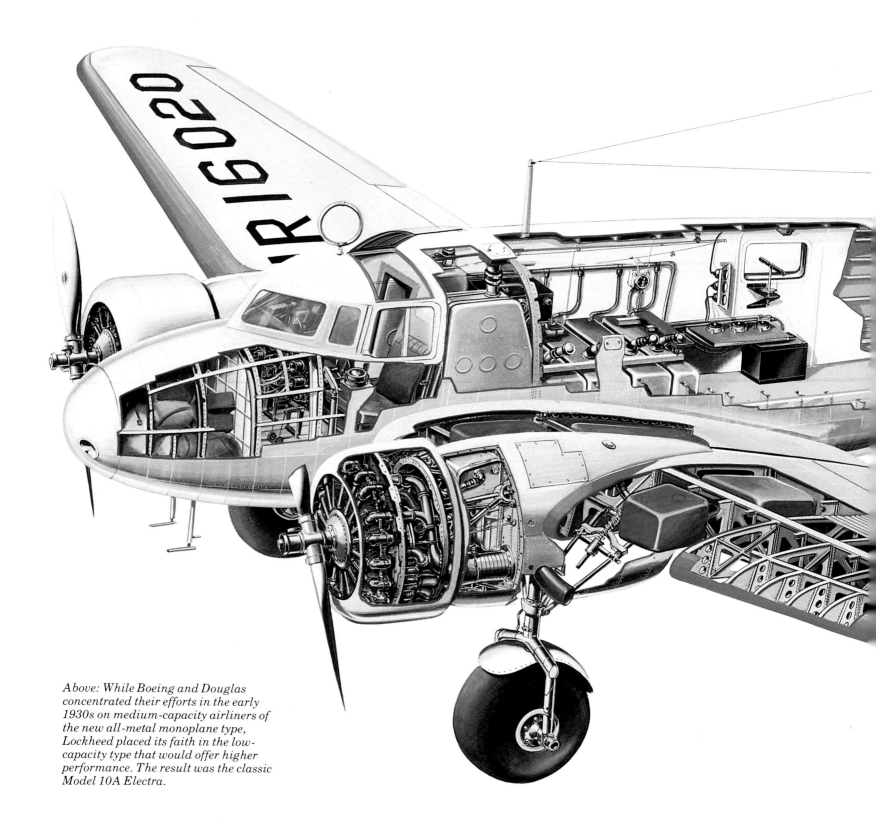

Above: While Boeing and Douglas concentrated their efforts in the early 1930s on medium-capacity airliners of the new all-metal monoplane type, Lockheed placed its faith in the low-capacity type that would offer higher performance. The result was the classic Model 10A Electra.

replaced by manually and then power operated turrets) and internal bomb bays. The USA and USSR went a step further with the development of their first modern multi-engined bombers for the long-range role: these aircraft presaged the strategic bomber of World War II.

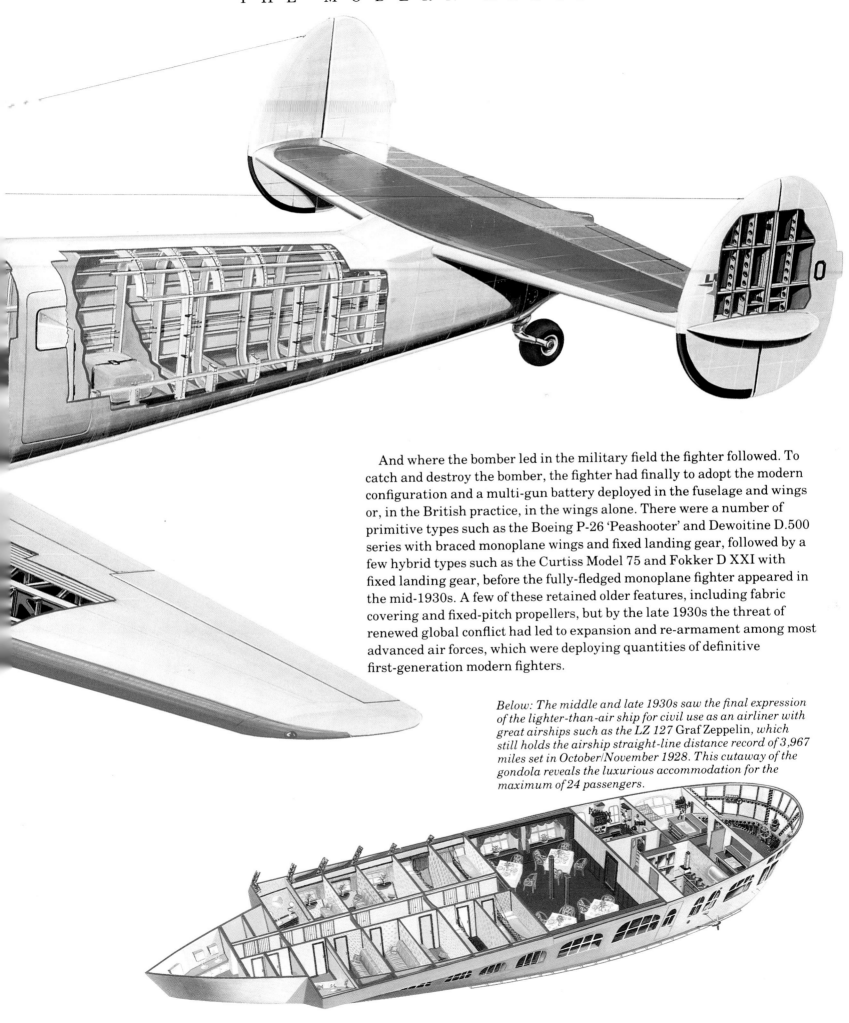

And where the bomber led in the military field the fighter followed. To catch and destroy the bomber, the fighter had finally to adopt the modern configuration and a multi-gun battery deployed in the fuselage and wings or, in the British practice, in the wings alone. There were a number of primitive types such as the Boeing P-26 'Peashooter' and Dewoitine D.500 series with braced monoplane wings and fixed landing gear, followed by a few hybrid types such as the Curtiss Model 75 and Fokker D XXI with fixed landing gear, before the fully-fledged monoplane fighter appeared in the mid-1930s. A few of these retained older features, including fabric covering and fixed-pitch propellers, but by the late 1930s the threat of renewed global conflict had led to expansion and re-armament among most advanced air forces, which were deploying quantities of definitive first-generation modern fighters.

Below: The middle and late 1930s saw the final expression of the lighter-than-air ship for civil use as an airliner with great airships such as the LZ 127 Graf Zeppelin, which still holds the airship straight-line distance record of 3,967 miles set in October/November 1928. This cutaway of the gondola reveals the luxurious accommodation for the maximum of 24 passengers.

Above: The Fairey Flycatcher was designed shortly after World War I for the first British generation of genuine aircraft-carriers, and despite its angular appearance combined with modest firepower and performance it remained in service into the early 1930s.

Left: Mainstay of the British fighter arm in the late 1920s and early 1930s, the Bristol Bulldog may have featured a metal airframe and modestly powerful radial engine, but remained faithful to fighter concept evolved in World War I in terms of configuration and firepower.

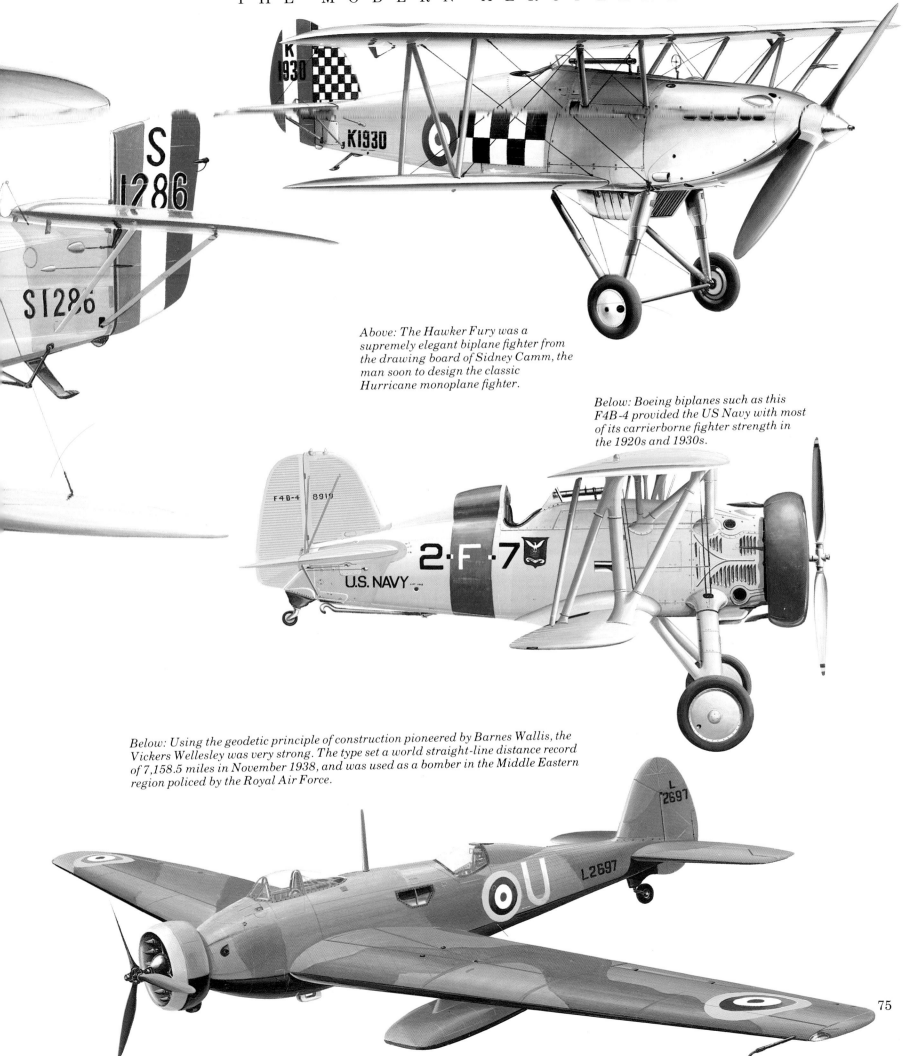

Above: The Hawker Fury was a supremely elegant biplane fighter from the drawing board of Sidney Camm, the man soon to design the classic Hurricane monoplane fighter.

Below: Boeing biplanes such as this F4B-4 provided the US Navy with most of its carrierborne fighter strength in the 1920s and 1930s.

Below: Using the geodetic principle of construction pioneered by Barnes Wallis, the Vickers Wellesley was very strong. The type set a world straight-line distance record of 7,158.5 miles in November 1938, and was used as a bomber in the Middle Eastern region policed by the Royal Air Force.

75

CHAPTER FIVE: WORLD WAR II

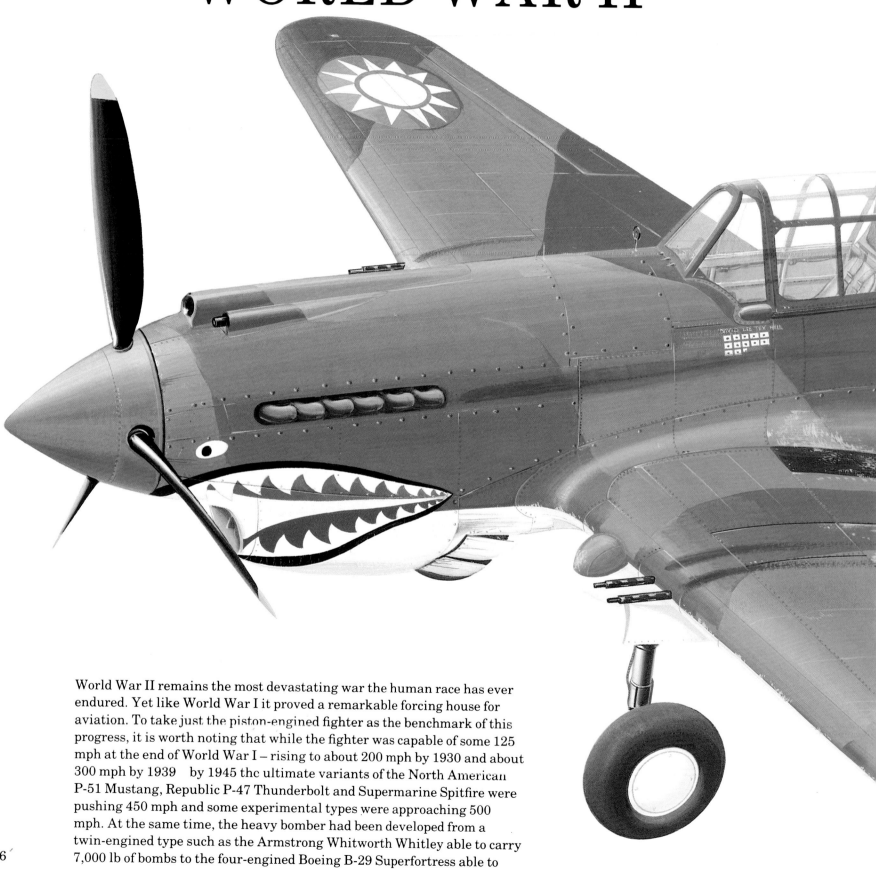

World War II remains the most devastating war the human race has ever endured. Yet like World War I it proved a remarkable forcing house for aviation. To take just the piston-engined fighter as the benchmark of this progress, it is worth noting that while the fighter was capable of some 125 mph at the end of World War I – rising to about 200 mph by 1930 and about 300 mph by 1939 by 1945 the ultimate variants of the North American P-51 Mustang, Republic P-47 Thunderbolt and Supermarine Spitfire were pushing 450 mph and some experimental types were approaching 500 mph. At the same time, the heavy bomber had been developed from a twin-engined type such as the Armstrong Whitworth Whitley able to carry 7,000 lb of bombs to the four-engined Boeing B-29 Superfortress able to

World War II was the conflict dominated by the type of fighter evolved in the late 1930s with a powerful engine in a cantilever monoplane airframe of all-metal construction with retractable landing gear. This Curtiss P-40 is typical of the breed, and is seen in the Chinese markings of the 'Flying Tigers', otherwise the American Volunteer Group.

carry 20,000 lb of bombs. The contrast is just as marked in the range and maximum speeds of the two bomber types, which were 1,500 and 3,250 miles, and 228 and 357 mph respectively. With machines such as these, in 1945, the piston-engined aeroplane reached its apogee in the military field and a successor was already entering the field – the turbojet. All this was achieved in a mere six years under the driving impetus of World War II.

Another factor that became emphasized in World War II was the differentiation of aircraft types, and the use of obsolescent types in secondary roles once they had begun to fade from prominence in their primary roles. This tendency was common to all of the combatants except the USA which had sufficient design and production resources to develop aircraft specifically for each role. Some US aircraft were indeed used for alternative roles, but this was basically because they displayed a particular capacity not because of dire necessity. The development of the air campaign in World War II also promoted the introduction of new aircraft categories, most notably the assault glider and its associated tug, the tactical transport and the night-fighter.

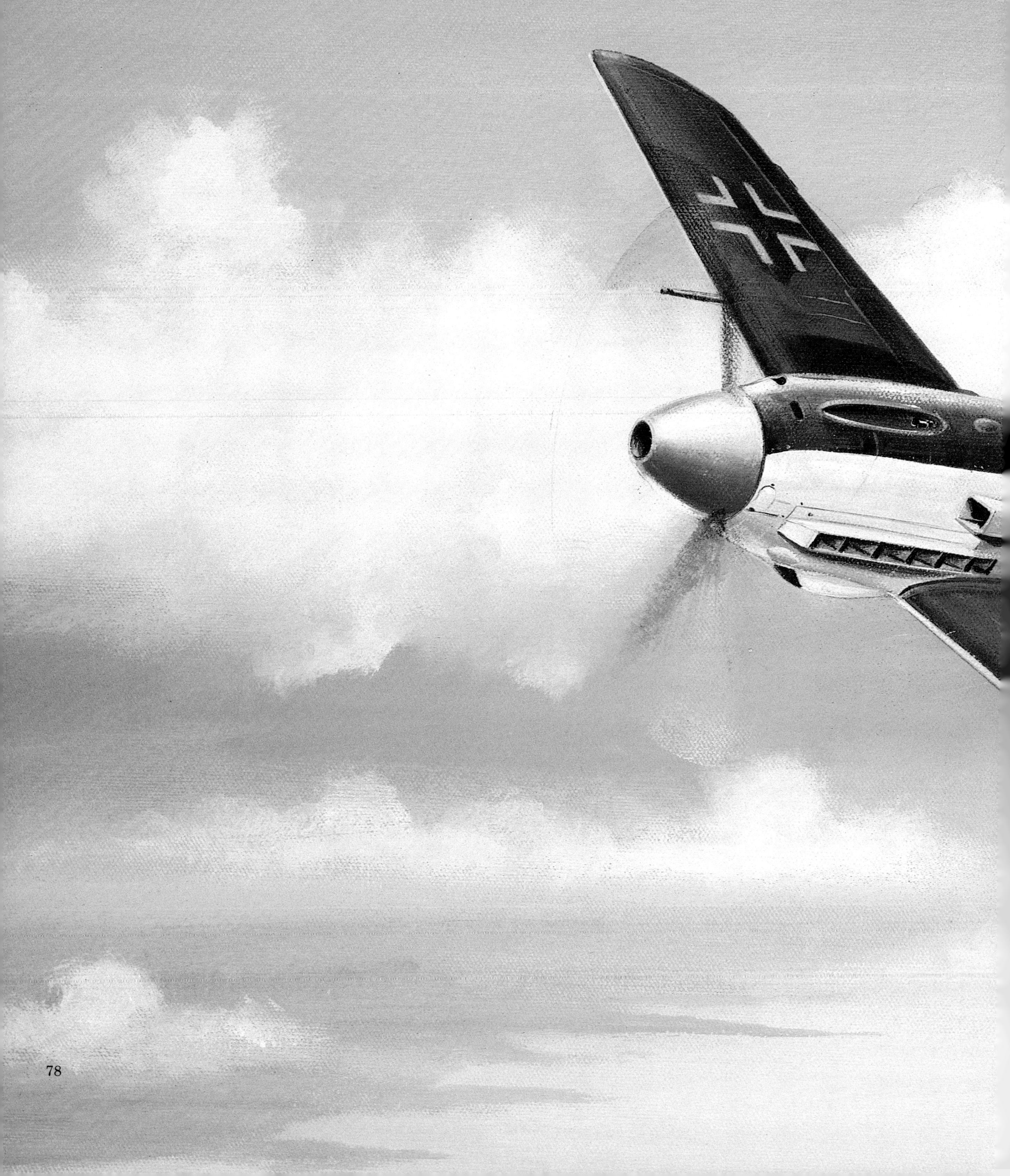

Pages 78— 9: Germany's most important fighter of World War II was the Messerschmitt Bf 109. This particular example is a Bf 109E of II/JG3 'Udet' (the second Gruppe or wing of the third Jagdgeschwader or fighter group) during 1940.

Pages 80— 1: The Bf 109's celebrated opponent was the Royal Air Force's most important fighter of World War II, the Supermarine Spitfire. This is a Spitfire Mk 1 of No.610 Squadron during 1940.

The single-engined fighters in service at the beginning of the war are epitomized by the British Spitfire Mk I and Hawker Hurricane Mk I, the French Morane-Saulnier M.S.406 and Dewoitine D.520 and the German Messerschmitt Bf 109E. The British fighters had eight rifle-calibre machine-guns, while the continental fighters generally had one 20-mm cannon and two rifle-calibre machine-guns. When the Italians and Americans came into the war later, their fighters were no match for these. However, the Italians were in the process of developing an open-cockpit monoplane fighter, the Fiat G.50, to replace the Fiat CR.32 and CR.42 biplanes, while another future German ally, Japan, was fielding light and exceptionally manoeuvrable retractable-gear monoplanes with radial engines in the form of the land-based Najakima Ki-43 and carrierborne Mitsubishi A6M – better known as the Zero – to supplement fixed-gear monoplanes such as the Nakajima Ki-27 and Mitsubishi A5M. On the other side of the political divide the Americans were introducing the Bell P-39 Airacobra and Curtiss P-40 Warhawk to replace the Seversky P-35 and Curtiss P-36, which were essentially interim types, and the Grumman F4F carrierborne fighter to replace the same company's F3F; the Americans were also developing more advanced types, most notably the Republic P-47 Thunderbolt, a massive aeroplane fitted with a turbocharger to wring the maximum horsepower out of the large radial engine. The USSR had developed the Polikarpov I-153, a version of the I-15 biplane fitted with retractable landing gear, and the Polikarpov I-16 monoplane. And a number of more advanced monoplanes were under development, including the Lavochkin LaGG-1, Mikoyan-Gurevich MiG-1 and Yakovlev Yak-1, all fitted with powerful inline engines and a mixed cannon and machine-gun armament.

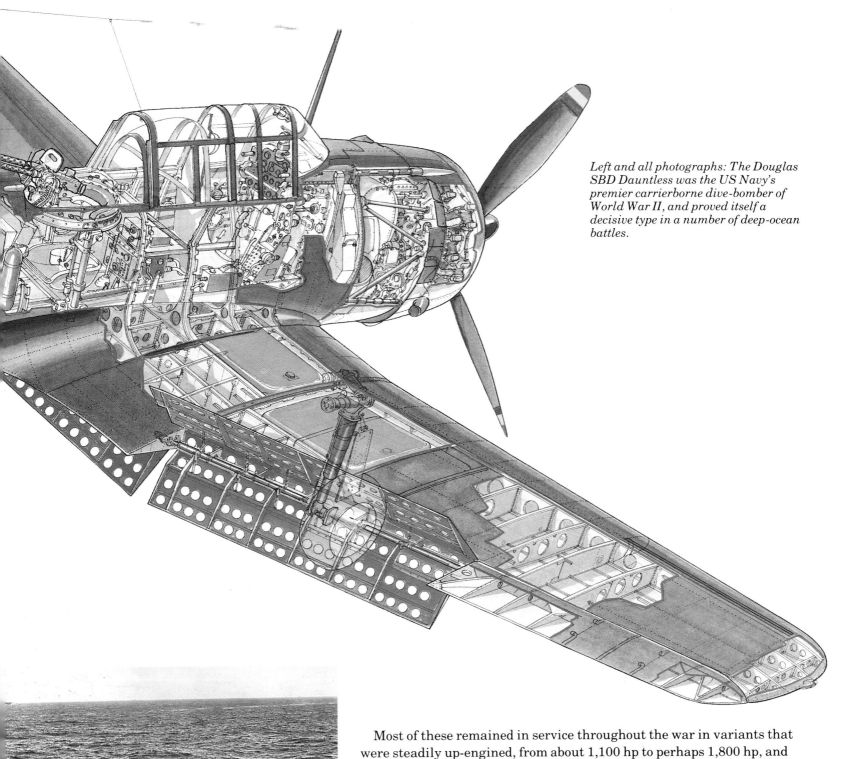

Left and all photographs: The Douglas SBD Dauntless was the US Navy's premier carrierborne dive-bomber of World War II, and proved itself a decisive type in a number of deep-ocean battles.

Most of these remained in service throughout the war in variants that were steadily up-engined, from about 1,100 hp to perhaps 1,800 hp, and up-armed to a British standard of two 20-mm cannon and four rifle-calibre machine-guns, a German standard of one 30-mm cannon and two heavy machine-guns often supplemented by two 20-mm cannon under the wings, and an American standard of six or eight heavy machine-guns. The Italians and Japanese also improved the armament of their fighters where possible, though it still remained light by contrast with that used in the fighters of more industrially advanced nations. The Soviets were generally content with the weight of the armament fitted to their fighters from the beginning and therefore restricted themselves mostly to improving the cannon. Many of these fighters though, were later given a ground-attack

83

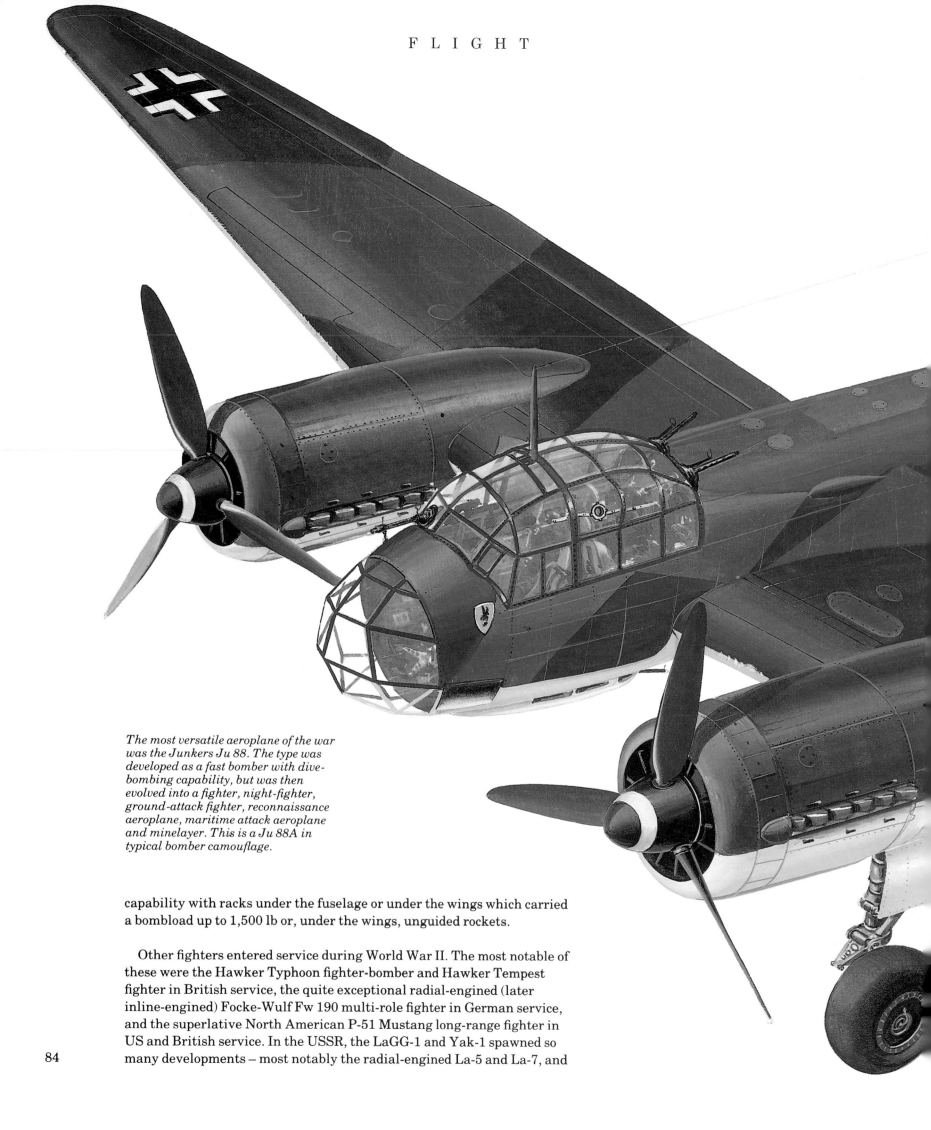

The most versatile aeroplane of the war was the Junkers Ju 88. The type was developed as a fast bomber with dive-bombing capability, but was then evolved into a fighter, night-fighter, ground-attack fighter, reconnaissance aeroplane, maritime attack aeroplane and minelayer. This is a Ju 88A in typical bomber camouflage.

capability with racks under the fuselage or under the wings which carried a bombload up to 1,500 lb or, under the wings, unguided rockets.

Other fighters entered service during World War II. The most notable of these were the Hawker Typhoon fighter-bomber and Hawker Tempest fighter in British service, the quite exceptional radial-engined (later inline-engined) Focke-Wulf Fw 190 multi-role fighter in German service, and the superlative North American P-51 Mustang long-range fighter in US and British service. In the USSR, the LaGG-1 and Yak-1 spawned so many developments – most notably the radial-engined La-5 and La-7, and

the inline-engined Yak-3, Yak-7 and Yak-9 – that can justifiably be called new aircraft. Italy and Japan also produced new fighters, some of them first-class machines. But they lacked the industrial base to build them in large numbers at a time that the tide of war was beginning to run against them.

In the late 1930s, there was something of a vogue for twin-engined fighters, which were seen as offering longer range than single-engined machines and the possibility of considerably heavier firepower. The Germans were the major exponents of the concept with the Messerschmitt

Bf 110, which was seen primarily as a bomber destroyer. Considerable development was undertaken before the war, but operationally the Bf 110 was deployed mainly as an escort, in which its range and firepower were indeed useful and compensated somewhat for its lack of agility. For this reason the Bf 110 was soon relegated to other tasks such as reconnaissance and, most importantly, night-fighting. In this arena, the Bf 110 did not have to 'mix it' with single-engined fighters, and had the payload capability to carry radar equipment which could be operated by the gunner.

The same concept was adopted by other countries, albeit in modified forms. The British first developed the potentially excellent Westland Whirlwind – a single-seat type that was cancelled because of engine

Among the many truly great warplanes developed by the United States of America for use in World War II, perhaps pride of place should go to the North American P-51 Mustang. This was developed to meet a British requirement, and once the original Allison engine had been replaced by a Packard-built Rolls-Royce Merlin as in this P-51D, the type emerged as a superlative long-range fighter that could escort bombers right into the heart of Germany.

limitations before more than a single production batch had been completed – then moved on to the classic two-seat Bristol Beaufighter. Like the Bf 110 in its later forms, this was first used as a night-fighter, but found its metier as a maritime strike fighter armed with a torpedo or rockets and bombs in addition to its mixed battery of cannon and machine-guns. The Americans' main twin-engined fighter was the single-seat Lockheed P-38 Lightning, an aerodynamically refined machine with a central nacelle for the pilot and armament plus twin booms stretching aft from the engines to contain the turbochargers and support the tailplane. Like other twin-engined fighters, the Lightning lacked the agility of single-seaters, but secured a significant niche for itself as a long-range fighter and reconnaissance aeroplane that won its successes largely by using the strength of the airframe for slashing dive and zoom attacks. The French and Italians also produced indifferent twin-engined fighters in small numbers, while the Japanese came to the concept relatively late but then made considerable strides in developing such machines for the task of intercepting the American heavy bombers that were burning the industrial heart out of Japan in 1944 and 1945.

In the early days of World War II, the British also tried converting Bristol Blenheim light bombers and the Douglas Havoc attack aircraft into twin-engined night-fighters. Other fighters were developed purely for the night-fighting role. The two finest were undoubtedly the Germans' Heinkel He 219 and the Americans' Northrop P-61 Black Widow, following the layouts of the Bf 110 and P-38 respectively. The Black Widow was a huge aeroplane. In addition to its fixed cannon has a remotely controlled barbette with four heavy machine-guns.

But Britain's most successful night-fighter of World War II was a variant of the de Havilland Mosquito, an extraordinary and beautiful aeroplane designed before the war as a private-venture light bomber. The design team planned the aeroplane with a structure based on de Havilland's well proved plywood/balsa sandwich method, with performance so high that no defensive armament would be needed. The type proved all that its designers planned, and more. The Mosquito was so full of development potential that it was evolved into a night-fighter,

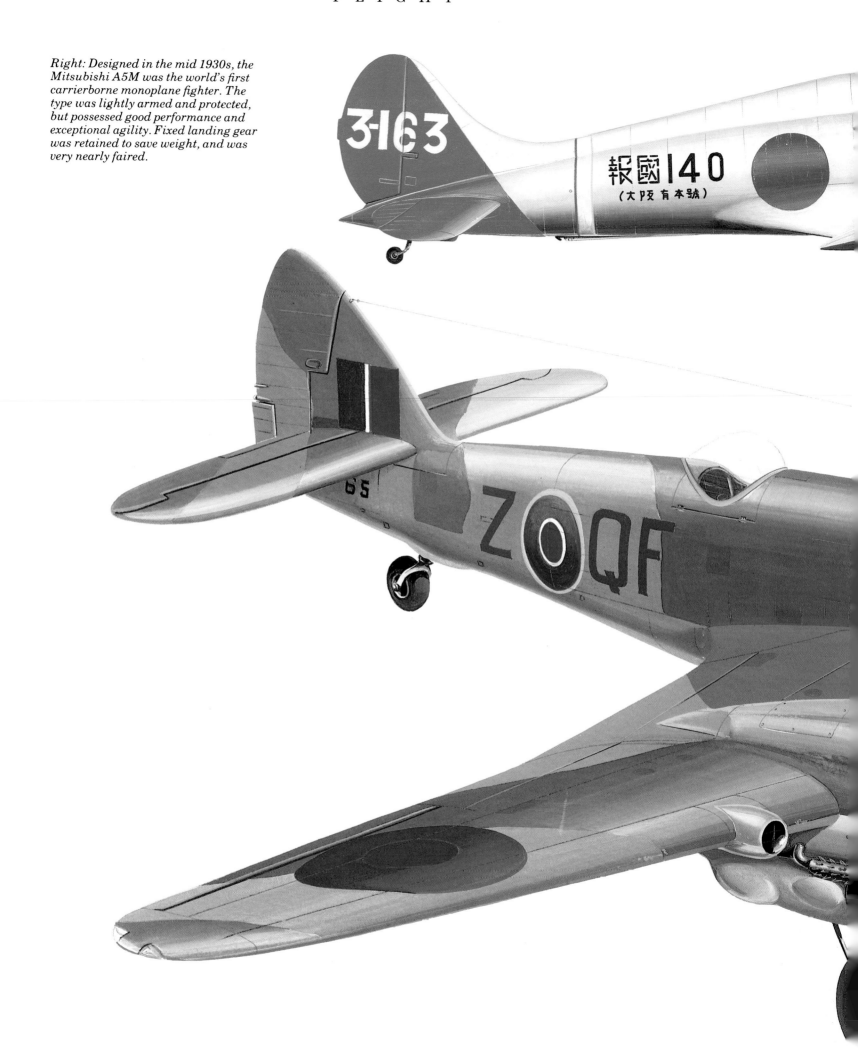

Right: Designed in the mid 1930s, the Mitsubishi A5M was the world's first carrierborne monoplane fighter. The type was lightly armed and protected, but possessed good performance and exceptional agility. Fixed landing gear was retained to save weight, and was very nearly faired.

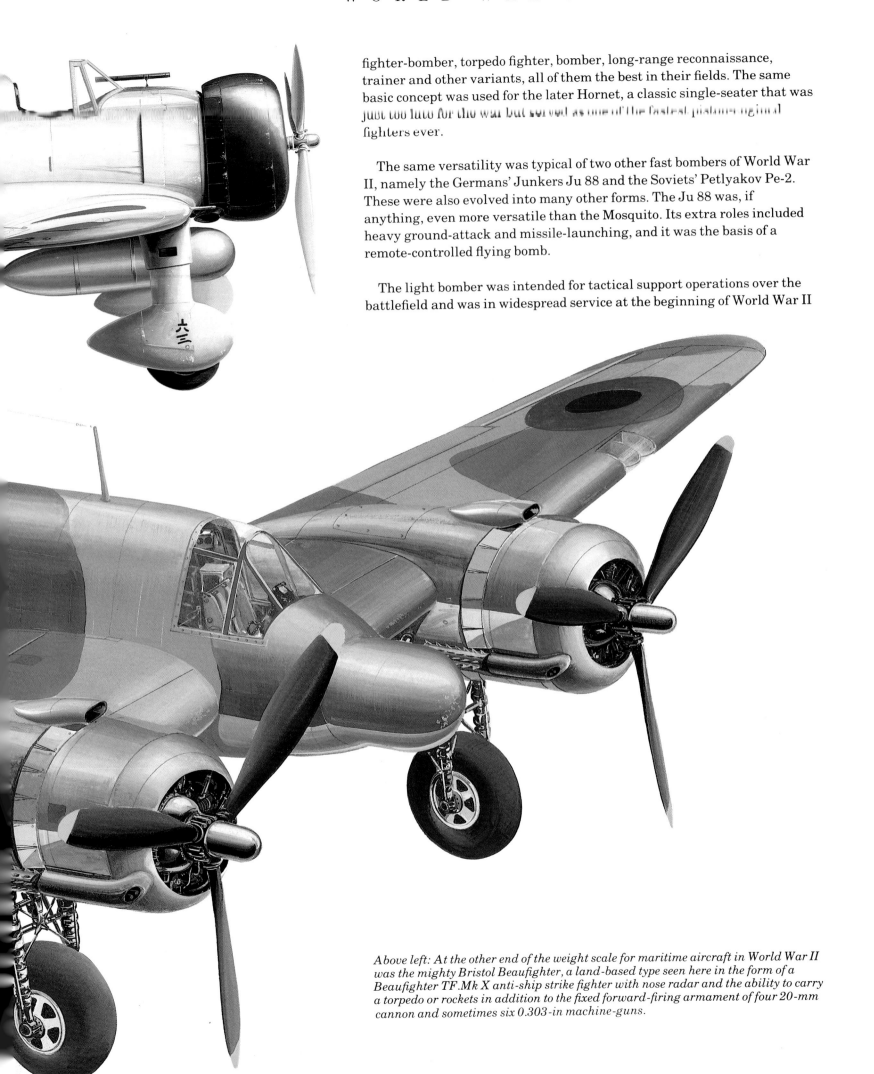

fighter-bomber, torpedo fighter, bomber, long-range reconnaissance,
trainer and other variants, all of them the best in their fields. The same
basic concept was used for the later Hornet, a classic single-seater that was
just too late for the war but served as one of the fastest piston-engined
fighters ever.

The same versatility was typical of two other fast bombers of World War
II, namely the Germans' Junkers Ju 88 and the Soviets' Petlyakov Pe-2.
These were also evolved into many other forms. The Ju 88 was, if
anything, even more versatile than the Mosquito. Its extra roles included
heavy ground-attack and missile-launching, and it was the basis of a
remote-controlled flying bomb.

The light bomber was intended for tactical support operations over the
battlefield and was in widespread service at the beginning of World War II

*Above left: At the other end of the weight scale for maritime aircraft in World War II
was the mighty Bristol Beaufighter, a land-based type seen here in the form of a
Beaufighter TF.Mk X anti-ship strike fighter with nose radar and the ability to carry
a torpedo or rockets in addition to the fixed forward-firing armament of four 20-mm
cannon and sometimes six 0.303-in machine-guns.*

89

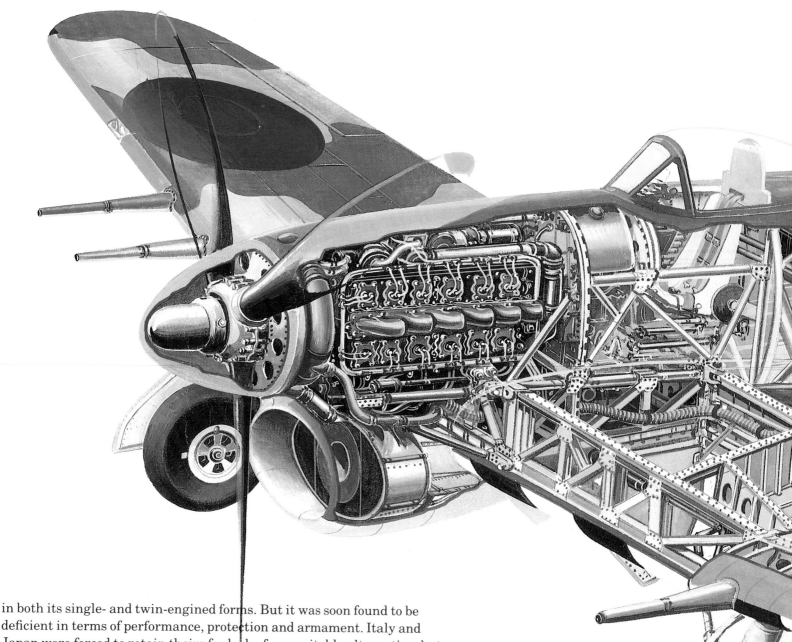

in both its single- and twin-engined forms. But it was soon found to be deficient in terms of performance, protection and armament. Italy and Japan were forced to retain theirs for lack of any suitable alternative, but the other combatants moved swiftly to the attack bomber with two powerful engines for high performance and a well-protected airframe that carried a heavy gun as well as bombs and often rockets. Germany experimented with several types but finally settled for a combination of fighter-bombers and ground-attack derivatives of existing twin-engined bombers. Britain followed a similar route. The Americans had the resources to produce two types, the Douglas A-20 Havoc and its successor, the Douglas B-26 Invader, to succeed to the miscellany of pre-war attack types still in service early in 1941. For the Soviets, the Pe-2 was the most important twin-engined attack bomber, but it was partnered by the single-engined Ilyushin Il-2 – more of these were built than any other war plane. This was initially a single-seater, but was then produced in two-seat form to become the most devastating attack aeroplane of World War II with its good handling, heavy protection and potent offensive/defensive armament. In 1944, the Soviets introduced the Tupolev Tu-2, one of the finest medium bombers and ground-attack aircraft of World War II. This twin-engined machine was successor to the Pe-2 and can be likened to the American B-25 and B-26 discussed below, but it was slightly smaller and perhaps better suited to the attack bomber than the medium bomber role.

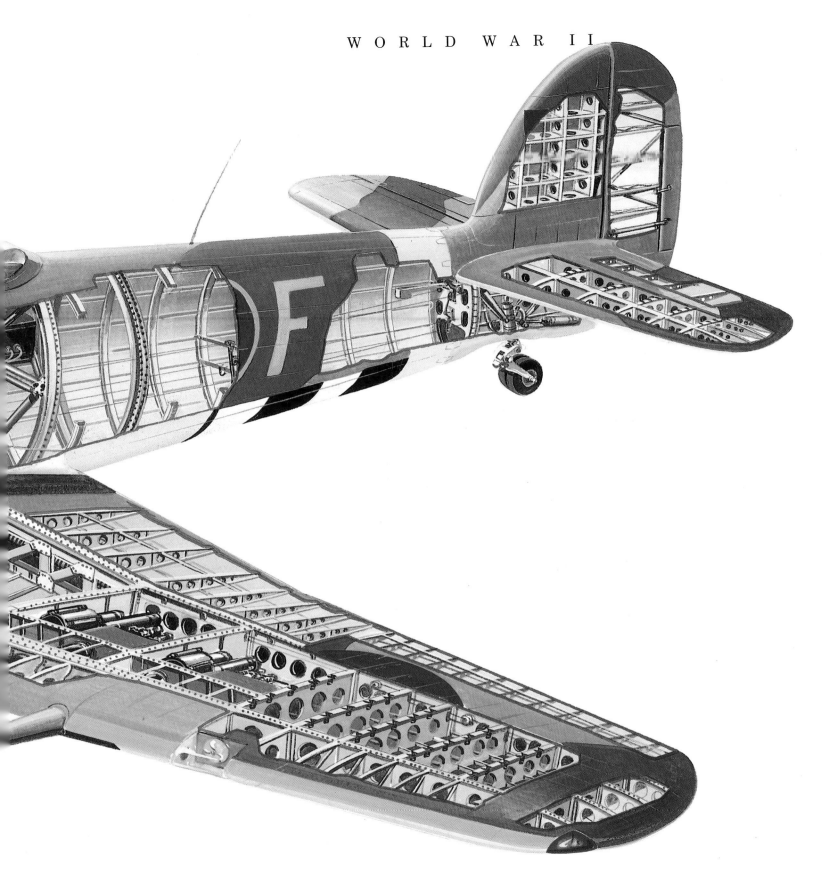

The Hawker Typhoon was designed as successor to the same company's Hurricane, but proved indifferent as an interceptor. Once problems with the tail had been eliminated, the type then matured as a magnificent ground-attack fighter in which the four 20-mm wing cannon were supplemented by eight rockets or two 500- or 1000-lb bombs carried under the wings.

The German counterpart to the Il-2 was the Junkers Ju 87, the dreaded *Stuka* that was synonymous with Germany's successful *Blitzkrieg* campaigns between 1939 and 1941. This was developed as a dive-bomber and initially used as such. But as this specifically tactical aeroplane became increasingly vulnerable to fighters and anti-aircraft guns it was adapted for ground attack and anti-tank work with specialist bombs and a pair of heavy anti-tank cannon under the wings. Despite the fact that it was completely obsolete by 1943, the Ju 87 was kept in service right up to 1945 in its ground attack variants and was the sole mount of World War II's most successful pilot, Hans-Ulrich Rudel.

Below: The heavyweight fighter fielded by the USA in World War II was the Republic P-47 Thunderbolt. The massive fuselage was dictated by the installation of a powerful radial engine in the nose and the weighty turbocharger in the rear fuselage, these two units being connected by ducting in the lower fuselage. This is an early P-47D from the period before a bubble canopy was introduced.

Tactical bombing at medium altitude was the preserve of the medium bomber, and while the Germans initially led in this field yet again, they were overtaken in the middle of the war by the Americans, whose vast design and production capabilities allowed them to develop more advanced types, then built them in the quantities sufficient to supply their allies as well as their own air force. Germany, on the other hand, had planned for a short war in which the ground forces would sweep all before them with the aid of a purely tactical air force. By the time the fallacy of this notion had

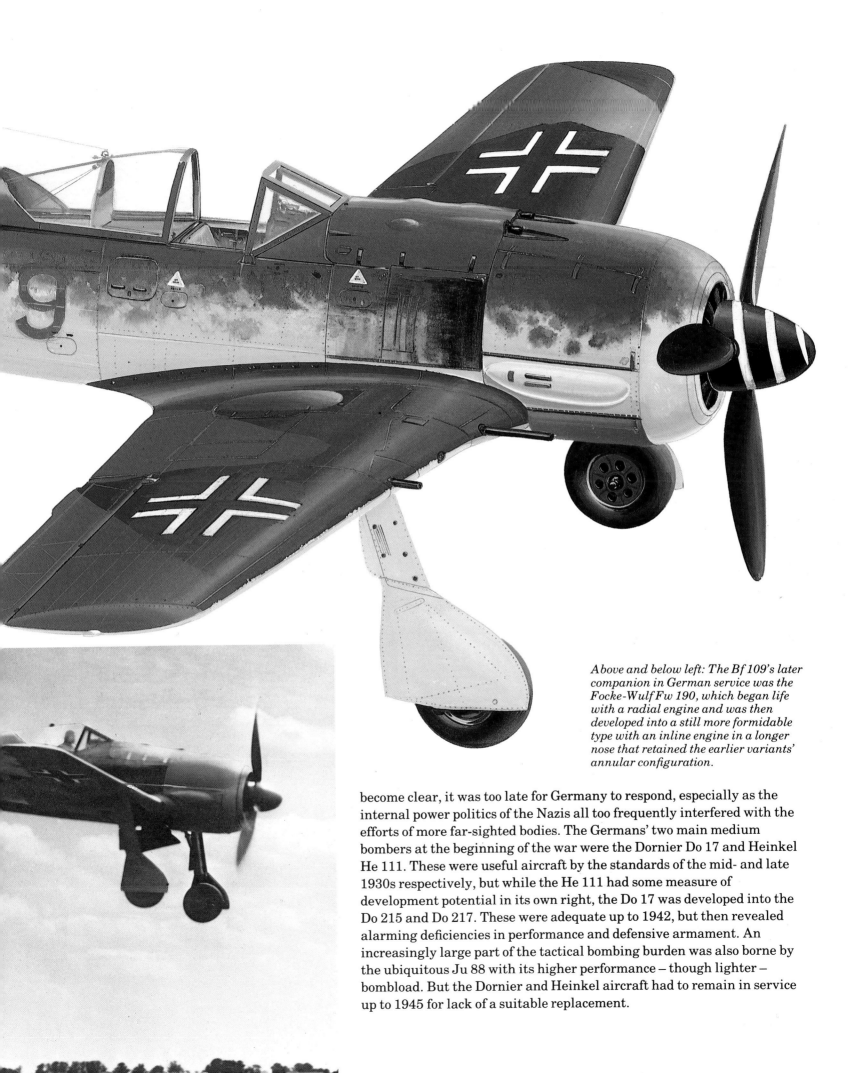

Above and below left: The Bf 109's later companion in German service was the Focke-Wulf Fw 190, which began life with a radial engine and was then developed into a still more formidable type with an inline engine in a longer nose that retained the earlier variants' annular configuration.

become clear, it was too late for Germany to respond, especially as the internal power politics of the Nazis all too frequently interfered with the efforts of more far-sighted bodies. The Germans' two main medium bombers at the beginning of the war were the Dornier Do 17 and Heinkel He 111. These were useful aircraft by the standards of the mid- and late 1930s respectively, but while the He 111 had some measure of development potential in its own right, the Do 17 was developed into the Do 215 and Do 217. These were adequate up to 1942, but then revealed alarming deficiencies in performance and defensive armament. An increasingly large part of the tactical bombing burden was also borne by the ubiquitous Ju 88 with its higher performance – though lighter – bombload. But the Dornier and Heinkel aircraft had to remain in service up to 1945 for lack of a suitable replacement.

93

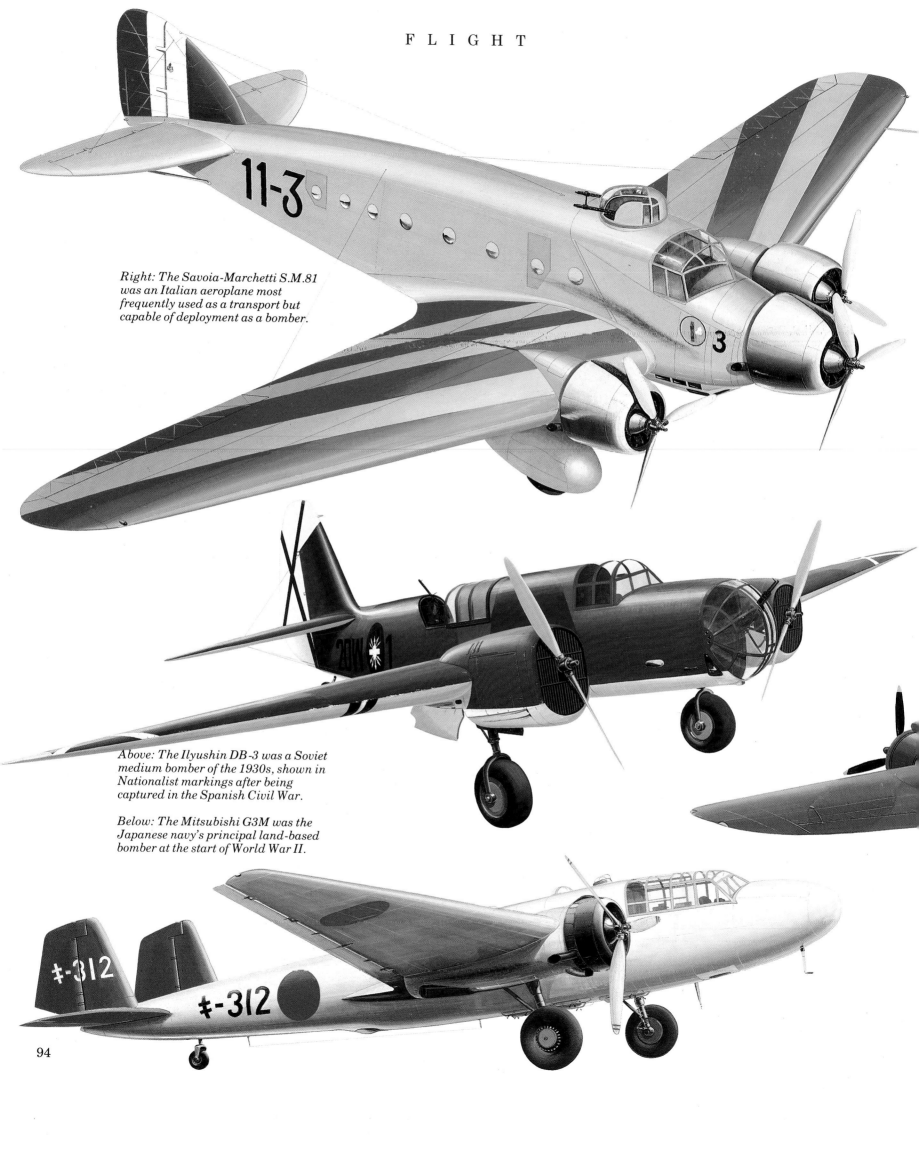

Right: The Savoia-Marchetti S.M.81 was an Italian aeroplane most frequently used as a transport but capable of deployment as a bomber.

Above: The Ilyushin DB-3 was a Soviet medium bomber of the 1930s, shown in Nationalist markings after being captured in the Spanish Civil War.

Below: The Mitsubishi G3M was the Japanese navy's principal land-based bomber at the start of World War II.

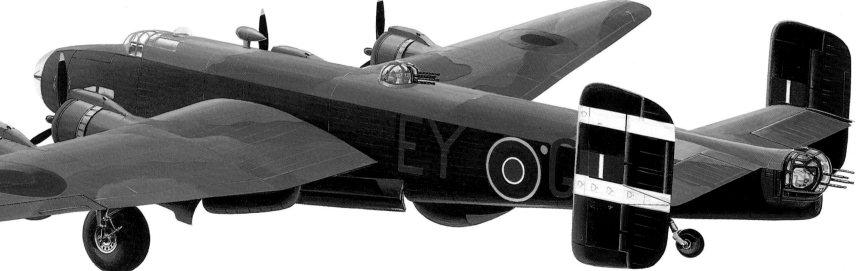

Top: The cockpit of the Handley Page Halifax.

Above: The Handley Page Halifax was developed with Bristol Hercules radial and Rolls-Royce Merlin inline engines, and though not as celebrated as the Avro Lancaster was still a very important component of the British night bombing effort in World War II.

The Americans' two main aircraft in this category were the North American B-25 Mitchell and Martin B-26 Marauder, both of them first-class machines. In common with most other American warplanes of World War II, these twin-engined medium bombers were powered by radial engines of great power and reliability, and the development potential of these engines was such that the designers could add steadily more armament and defensive armour to the B-25 and B-26 in the full confidence that performance would not be degraded to any significant degree. Both machines were fitted with tricycle landing gear and, by contrast with the Germans bombers which concentrated their crews in a

95

3455

J. BATCHELOR

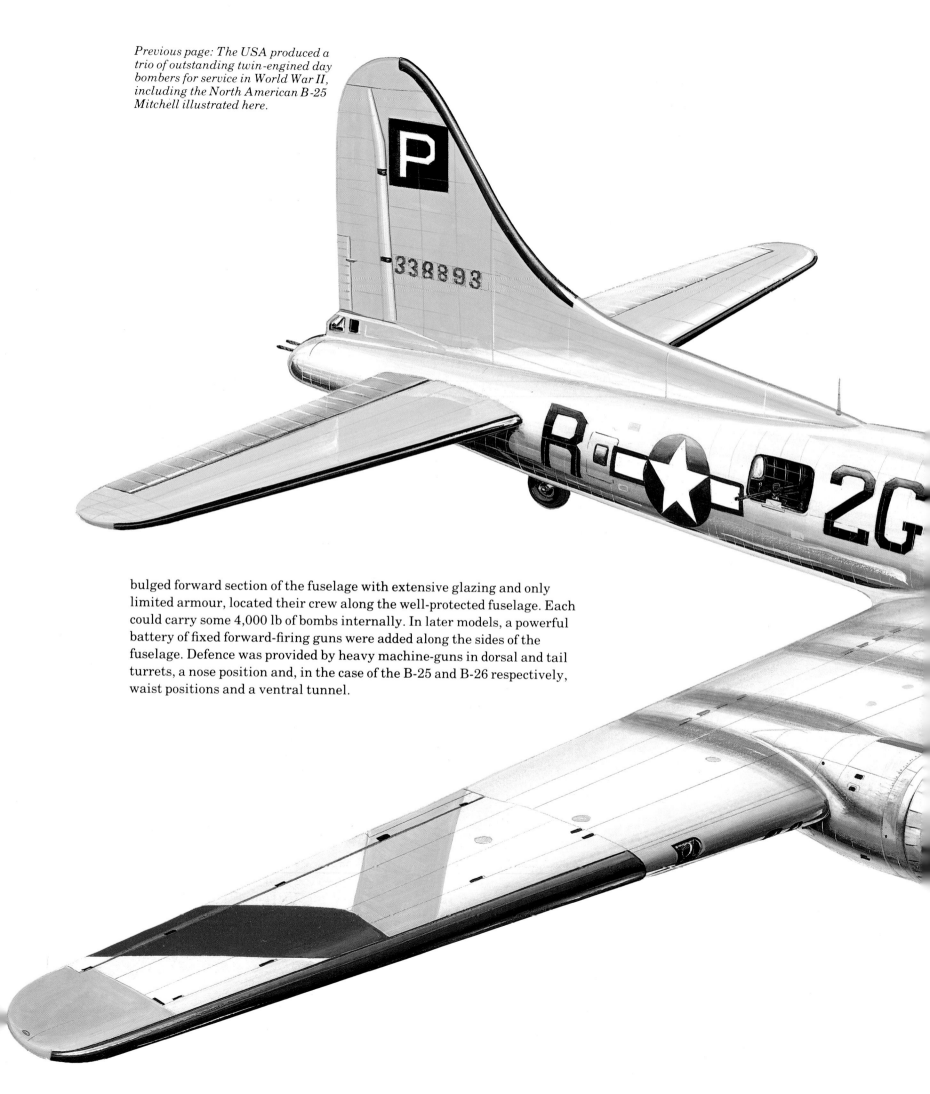

Previous page: The USA produced a trio of outstanding twin-engined day bombers for service in World War II, including the North American B-25 Mitchell illustrated here.

bulged forward section of the fuselage with extensive glazing and only limited armour, located their crew along the well-protected fuselage. Each could carry some 4,000 lb of bombs internally. In later models, a powerful battery of fixed forward-firing guns were added along the sides of the fuselage. Defence was provided by heavy machine-guns in dorsal and tail turrets, a nose position and, in the case of the B-25 and B-26 respectively, waist positions and a ventral tunnel.

*The American heavy bomber that
served with the greatest distinction in
the European theatre was the Boeing
B-17 Flying Fortress. This is a B-17G
with the chin turret added to deter the
German fighters which had found the
head-on attack to offer the best chance
of downing earlier variants.*

The Japanese operated a number of twin-engined bombers with
comparable performance and bombload, most notably the Mitsubishi
Ki-21, G3M and G4M. These were deemed to be heavy bombers but lacked
the armour and prodigious gunpower of the American bombers. Like the
Americans, the Japanese used radial engines as the main powerplant
types for their fighters and bombers. But unlike the Americans they lacked
the massive production rate of constantly improved engines that might

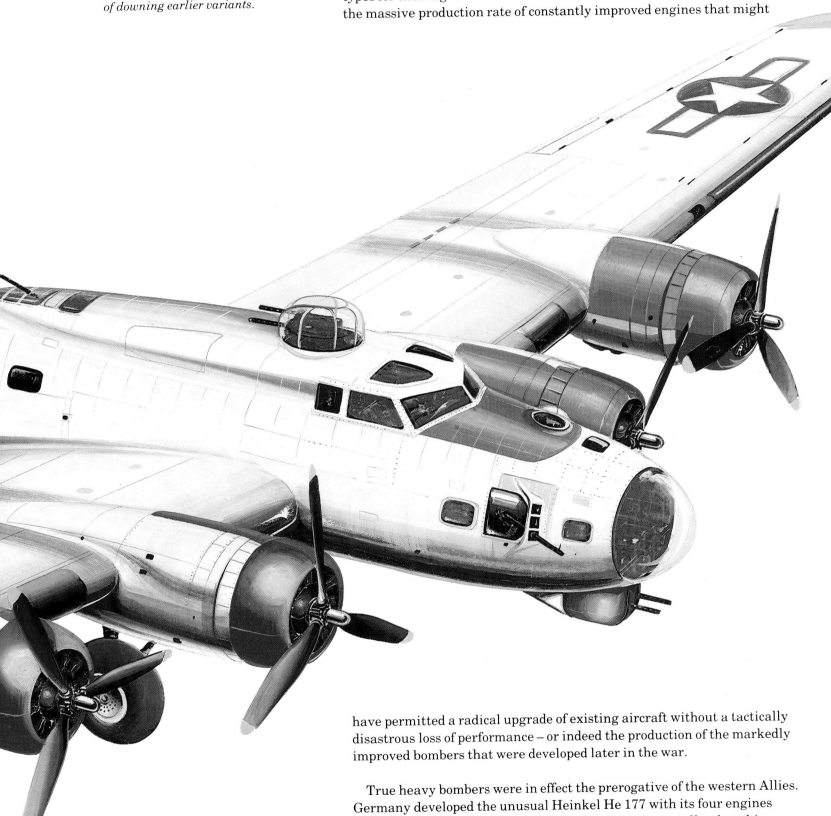

have permitted a radical upgrade of existing aircraft without a tactically
disastrous loss of performance – or indeed the production of the markedly
improved bombers that were developed later in the war.

   True heavy bombers were in effect the prerogative of the western Allies.
Germany developed the unusual Heinkel He 177 with its four engines
coupled into pairs each driving a single four-blade propeller, but this
potentially useful aeroplane was hampered by the unreliability of its
powerplant. Italy developed the four-engined Piaggio P.108 that was

99

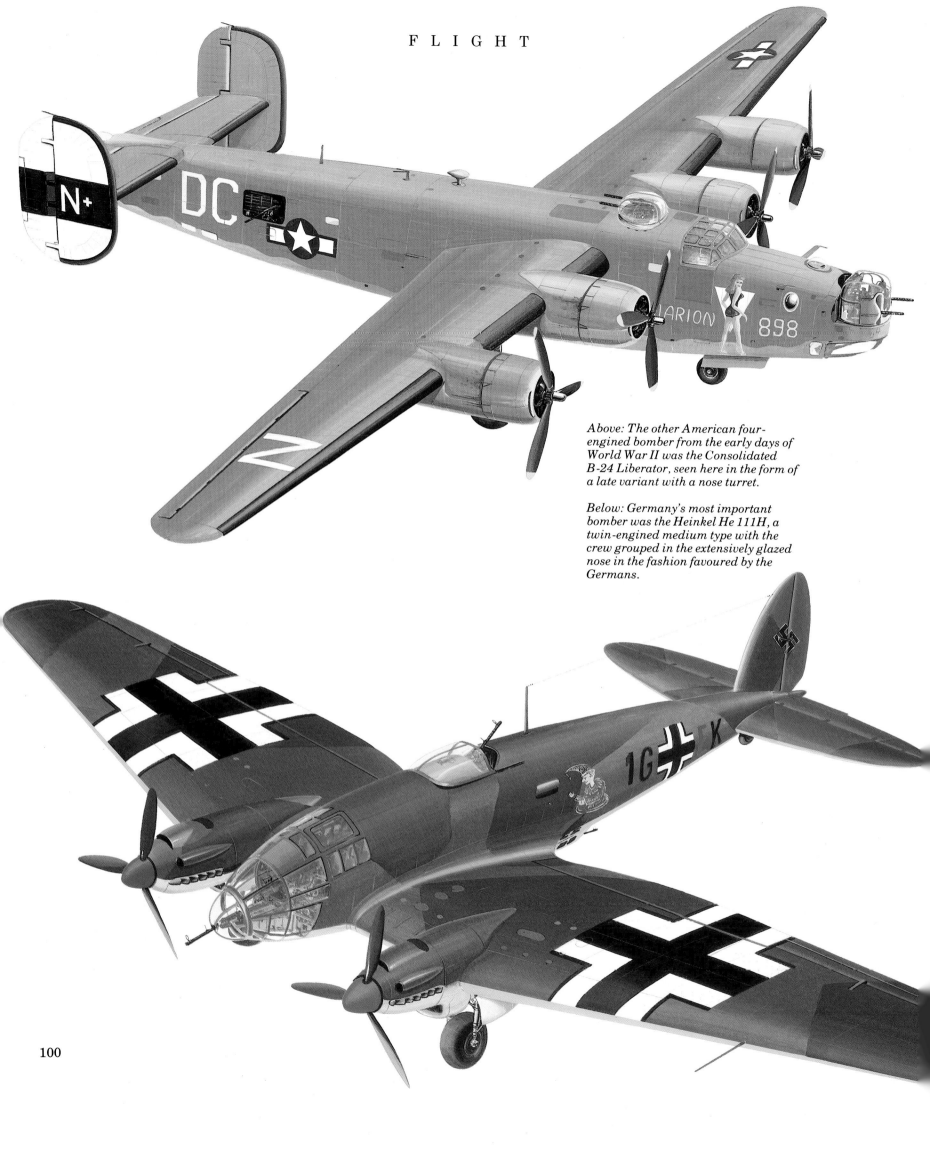

Above: The other American four-engined bomber from the early days of World War II was the Consolidated B-24 Liberator, seen here in the form of a late variant with a nose turret.

Below: Germany's most important bomber was the Heinkel He 111H, a twin-engined medium type with the crew grouped in the extensively glazed nose in the fashion favoured by the Germans.

produced in small numbers. Japan also sought to produce a long-range bomber with the range to bomb the USA from Japan, but failed to get any into production. And on the Allied side the USSR had the Petlyakov Pe-8, a useful heavy bomber of some potential, but which was produced only in small numbers. This marks an odd reversal of emphasis. During the 1930s great effort had been devoted to the creation of a heavy bomber forces with aircraft such as the Tupolev TB-3. But the Soviet air effort in World War II was devoted almost exclusively to tactical support of the ground forces.

First in the field with a genuine heavy bomber were the Americans with the Boeing B-17 Fortress and slightly later Consolidated B-24 Liberator.

Above: The Messerschmitt Bf 110 was an indifferent heavy day fighter, but was then developed into a potent radar-fitted night fighter as typified by this Bf 110G.

Below: The best bomber available to the British at the beginning of World War II was the Vickers Wellington, and this type remained in service in many variants right to the end of the War switching initially to the night bomber and then maritime reconnaissance roles.

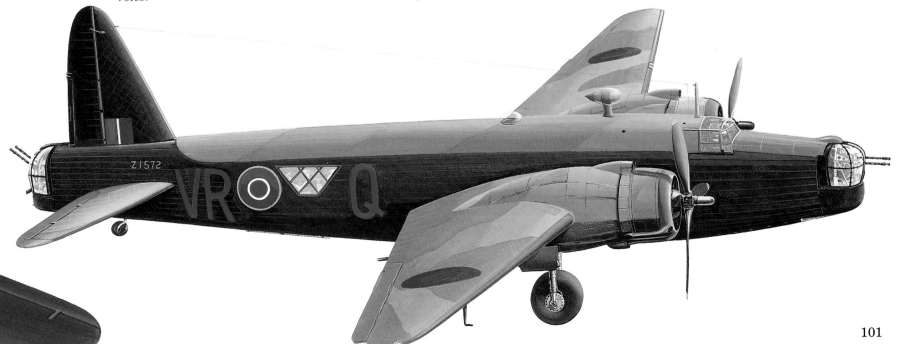

The American concept of heavy bombing was centred on the notion of destroying key industries and communications by concentrated but accurate bombing from high altitude. This demanded operation by day, and the two American bombers offered good performance at altitude, a moderately heavy bombload and, in the case of the B-24, excellent range. Both models were improved through several variants in World War II, the emphasis being mainly on better protection and gun armament. The B-24 was given heavy, rather than rifle-calibre, machine-guns and additional guns including two in a new nose turret to provide a defence against the head-on engagements used by German and Japanese fighter pilots. The ultimate heavy bomber of World War II, however, was the Boeing B-29 Superfortress, the long-range type that took the strategic air war to Japan and ultimately dropped the A-bombs on Hiroshima and Nagasaki during August 1945, ending the war. At the purely technical level, the B-29 was an enormous achievement with remotely controlled gun barbettes, pressurized crew compartments for high-altitude operation over long ranges, and mighty turbocharged engines for high speed at high altitude. The Soviets secured three B-29s forced to land in Siberia. They were so impressed that they copied them in the Tu-4, the starting point for much of the USSR's post-war development of strategic bombers.

Britain started the war with a trio of twin-engined 'heavy' bombers in the Armstrong Whitworth Whitley, the Handley Page Hampden and the Vickers Wellington. Losses of these aircraft to German fighters soon forced the British to adopt the concept of diffuse night bombing of area targets. The Whitley and Hampden lasted only into the beginning of the war, but the Wellington proved a sturdier beast capable of considerable development as a medium night bomber. It thus remained a first-line aircraft until the end of the war, though it was increasingly shifted to secondary roles such as maritime reconnaissance. The first 'modern' heavy bomber accepted by the RAF was the Avro Manchester, but this twin-engined machine was let down by its unreliable powerplant and replaced by the superlative Lancaster with four of the inline engine that

The Northrop P-61 Black Widow was a massive American night fighter with nose radar, four 20-mm fixed cannon and, in some models, an upper-fuselage barbette carrying four 0.5-in machine-guns.

Japan's most important fighter of World War II was the Mitsubishi A6M, a carrierborne type known to the Allies as the Zero or by its official reporting name of Zeke. The type remained in development and service throughout the War, but was outmoded by Allied standards from 1943.

powered so many great British warplanes of period (along with the definitive version of the American P-51 Mustang), namely the Rolls-Royce Merlin. The Lancaster remained the mainstay of Bomber Command right through the war. The generally similar Lincoln developed to replace it entered service only after the war. But the Lancaster was only one of a trio of British four-engined heavy bombers. The first of these was the Short Stirling. Designed to fit into existing hangars, its small wings so affected its ceiling that the Stirling's life as a bomber was short. It then went on to a successful second career as an airborne forces' aeroplane. The other British four-engined bomber was the Handley Page Halifax, an altogether more successful type that partnered the Lancaster through the second half of the war. It was also used in important maritime reconnaissance and airborne forces roles.

The other main task for many shore-based aircraft was maritime reconnaissance and the related anti-ship and anti-submarine roles. It was common for longer-ranged bombers – like the Halifax and the Liberator – to be fitted out for the maritime reconnaissance role, while the Germans developed a version of the Focke-Wulf Fw 200 Condor airliner for this task. Medium bombers also featured in conversion programmes to develop torpedo bombers of useful range – the Hampden and He 111 are good examples alongside perhaps the best land-based torpedo bomber of World War II, the Savoia-Marchetti S.M.79 Sparviero used by the Italian air force. But specialist maritime reconnaissance and torpedo bombing aircraft were also produced. Good examples of the land-based varieties were the Consolidated PB2Y Privateer (a radical development of the Liberator), the Junkers Ju 290 patrol aircraft and the Bristol Beaufort

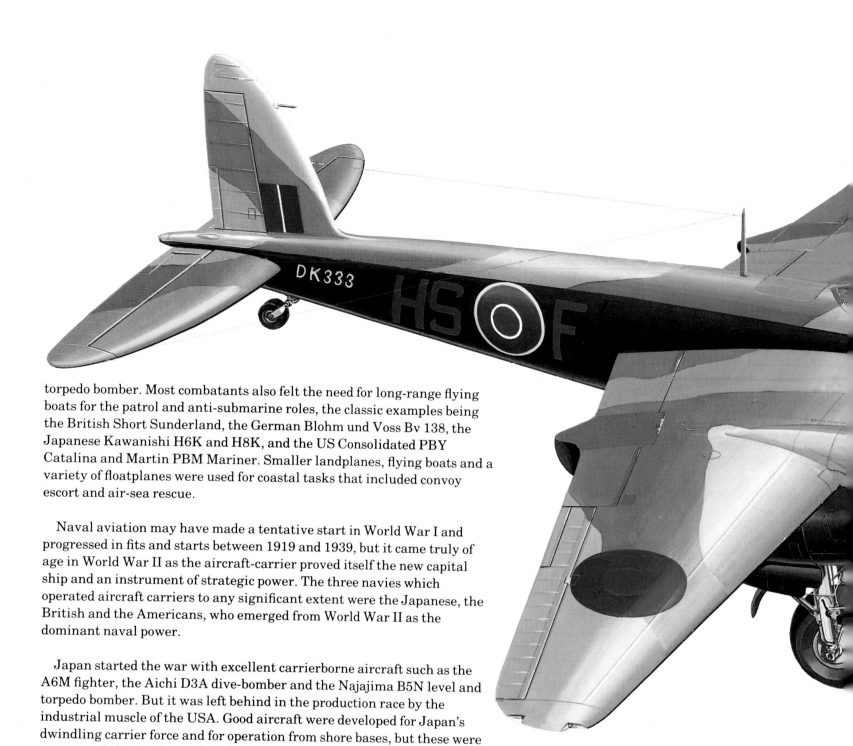

torpedo bomber. Most combatants also felt the need for long-range flying boats for the patrol and anti-submarine roles, the classic examples being the British Short Sunderland, the German Blohm und Voss Bv 138, the Japanese Kawanishi H6K and H8K, and the US Consolidated PBY Catalina and Martin PBM Mariner. Smaller landplanes, flying boats and a variety of floatplanes were used for coastal tasks that included convoy escort and air-sea rescue.

Naval aviation may have made a tentative start in World War I and progressed in fits and starts between 1919 and 1939, but it came truly of age in World War II as the aircraft-carrier proved itself the new capital ship and an instrument of strategic power. The three navies which operated aircraft carriers to any significant extent were the Japanese, the British and the Americans, who emerged from World War II as the dominant naval power.

Japan started the war with excellent carrierborne aircraft such as the A6M fighter, the Aichi D3A dive-bomber and the Najajima B5N level and torpedo bomber. But it was left behind in the production race by the industrial muscle of the USA. Good aircraft were developed for Japan's dwindling carrier force and for operation from shore bases, but these were never available in time or in sufficient numbers to affect the course of the naval war in the Pacific.

Britain started the war with obsolescent aircraft such as the Blackburn Roc turret fighter, the Blackburn Skua dive-bomber and the Fairey Swordfish torpedo bomber. Oddly enough, it was the slow biplane, the Swordfish, that remained in service right through the war, proving a capable and versatile machine that outlived its successor, the Fairey Albacore. Other aircraft were developed in the form of the Fairey Barracuda torpedo bomber, the Fairey Fulmar fighter and the far superior Fairey Firefly fighter and reconnaissance aeroplane, but it proved so difficult to produce a naval fighter effective enough to tackle land-based fighters that a carrierborne Seafire was derived from the Spitfire before the Hawker Sea Fury arrived just too late for the war.

The British counterpart to the German Ju 88 was the de Havilland Mosquito, built largely of a balsa/plywood sandwich material and seen here in the form of a Mosquito B.Mk IV of the original high-speed bomber variant.

British aircraft-carriers made extensive use of the magnificent range of American carrierborne aircraft developed in the late 1930s and early 1940s. At the time of Pearl Harbor in December 1941, a new generation of aircraft was coming forward to replace the US Navy's standard Brewster F2A fighter, Douglas TBD Devastator torpedo bomber and the Northrop BT dive-bomber. These included the Grumman F4F Wildcat fighter, the Grumman TBF Avenger level and torpedo bomber, and the Douglas SBD Dauntless dive-bomber. The F4F was superseded from 1943 by the F6F Hellcat fighter and fighter-bomber, itself supplemented in 1945 by the F8F Bearcat interceptor, while the TBF remained in service and development until well after the war. The SBD was overtaken by the Curtiss SB2C Helldiver as a scout and dive-bomber. To these must be added the Vought F4U Corsair, a type that has some claim to the distinction of being the best fighter – and certainly fighter-bomber – of the war. Initially rejected for carrierborne operations, the Corsair was used as a land-based aircraft until introduced on the Royal Navy's carriers, whereupon it was finally accepted by the US Navy for carrierborne deployment.

The airborne deployment of troops became virtually conventional in World War II, after being initially pioneered by the Germans. The two main types of aircraft used were assault gliders and paratroop transports that often doubled as glider tugs. The main assault gliders of the war were the British Airspeed Horsa and General Aircraft Hamilcar, the German DFS 230 and Gotha Go 242, and the US Waco CG-4 Hadrian. A number of superannuated bombers were employed by the British and Germans as glider tugs, though the Germans also made extensive use of the Junkers Ju 52/3m transport as a tug and also as a paratrooping aeroplane. The US counterpart to these was the superlative Douglas C-47, often called the Dakota and essentially the militarized version of the DC-3 airliner.

Air transport was also needed. Again converted bombers had their part to play, and the Germans also produced a number of development types that were used in small numbers, including the huge Messerschmitt Me 321 glider and the six-engined Me 323 powered version. But the nation that brought air transport to a high peak of capability was the USA. In addition to the C-47, it used another twin-engined type, the Curtiss-Wright C-46 Commando, in the Far East, and pressed into service two airliners that were under development at the beginning of the war. These were the Douglas DC-4 and Lockheed L-049 Constellation that were used by the military as the C-54 Skymaster and C-69 respectively.

World War II also marked a completely new departure in aircraft with the service debut of the world's first turbojet-powered warplanes. The first jet-powered aeroplane was the Heinkel He 178 that flew as early as August 1939, but convinced that the war would be short, and won by existing types of aircraft, Germany then slowed all further development. It was the British who brought into service the world's first operational jet-powered warplane, the Gloster Meteor fighter, during July 1944, just a few days before the more advanced Messerschmitt Me 262 fighter. The only other operational jet of World War II was another German machine, the Arado Ar 234 bomber and reconnaissance aeroplane, but only a few of these entered service. Had the war lasted longer there might have been several more, for German technology had produced other prototypes, while the British were flying the first examples of the de Havilland Vampire, and the Americans had produced small numbers of two fighters, the indifferent Bell P-59 Airacomet and the first-class Lockheed P-80 Shooting Star.

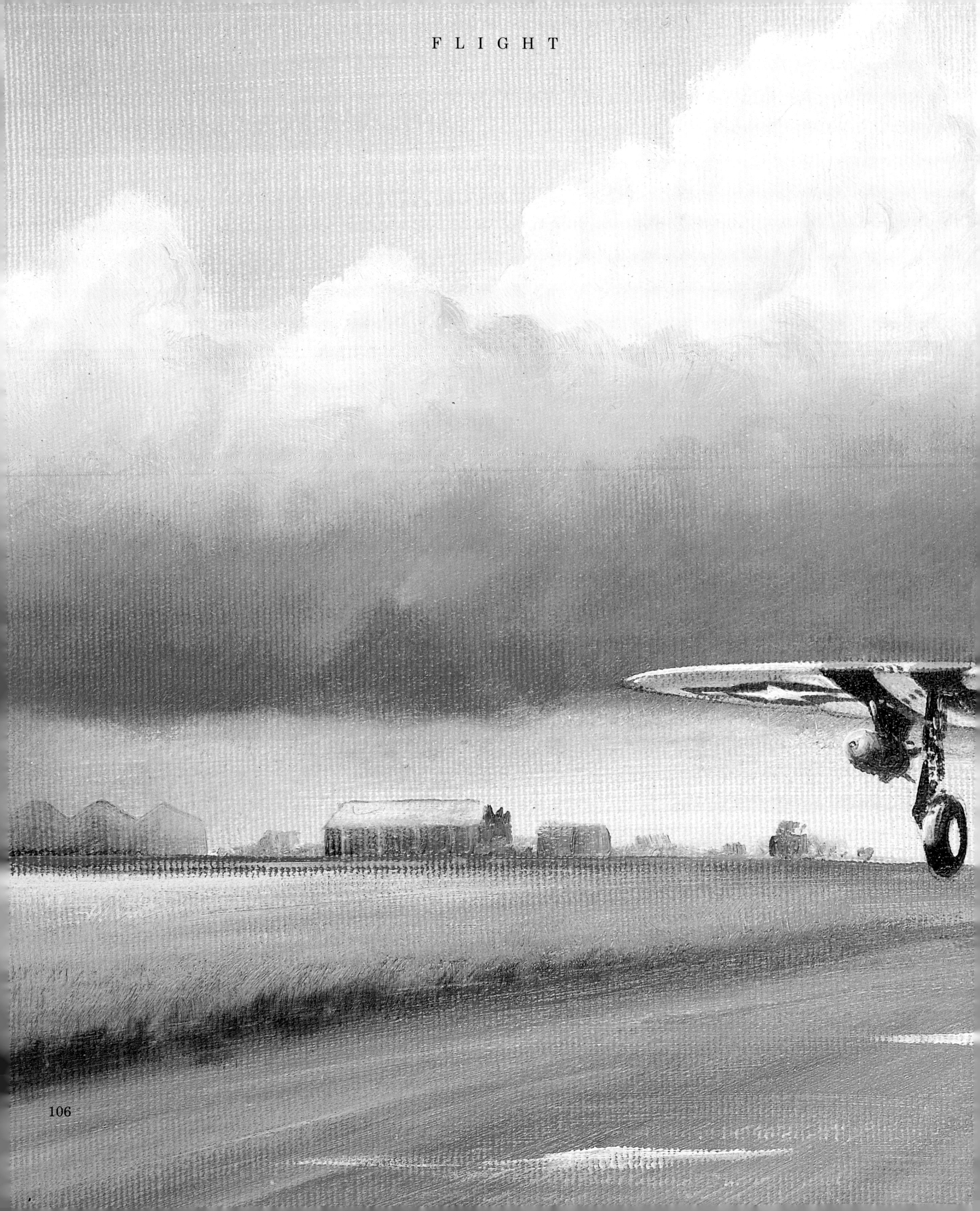

CHAPTER SIX: THE JET AGE

At the end of World War II aviation was at the door of the jet age. Germany, Britain and America had each developed combat-capable jet warplanes, while Japan and the USSR were slightly further behind. More important in the longer term, however, was the vast amount of research that the Germans had undertaken in all aspects of jet-powered flight at high subsonic speeds. Axial-flow turbojets and advanced aerodynamics were the two most important aspects of this effort, and the German

Previous page: An evocative painting catches a Republic P-47D Thunderbolt fighter-bomber departing on a ground-attack mission in its black/white-striped D-Day markings and carrying two underwing bombs to supplement its fixed armament of eight 0.5-in machine-guns.

research data were eagerly seized by the Allies along with complete aircraft, their engines and even their designers. For the most part the German research was far ahead of the Allied equivalent, and the years immediately after the war were marked by a frantic effort to assimilate the German research into the jet aircraft programmes of the USA and USSR. As had been the case after World War I, Britain was nearly bankrupt, and its government decided that so high-powered a technological effort was beyond British resources.

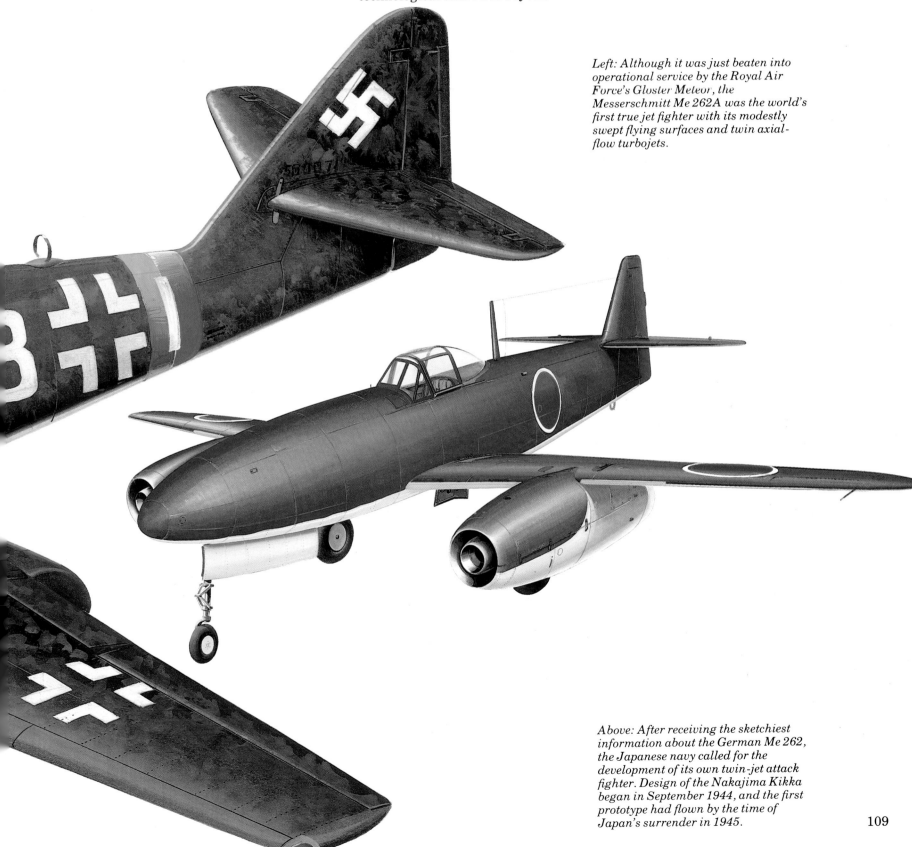

Left: Although it was just beaten into operational service by the Royal Air Force's Gloster Meteor, the Messerschmitt Me 262A was the world's first true jet fighter with its modestly swept flying surfaces and twin axial-flow turbojets.

Above: After receiving the sketchiest information about the German Me 262, the Japanese navy called for the development of its own twin-jet attack fighter. Design of the Nakajima Kikka began in September 1944, and the first prototype had flown by the time of Japan's surrender in 1945.

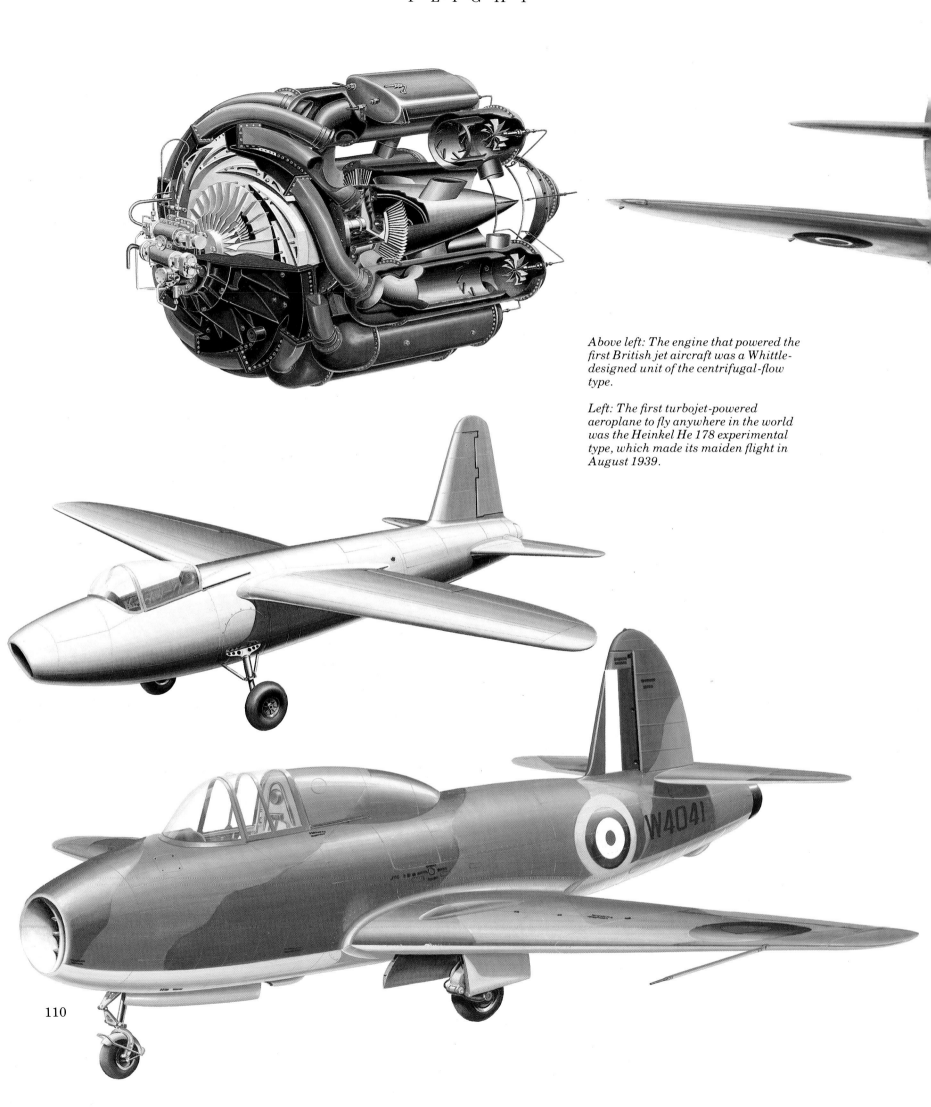

Above left: The engine that powered the first British jet aircraft was a Whittle-designed unit of the centrifugal-flow type.

Left: The first turbojet-powered aeroplane to fly anywhere in the world was the Heinkel He 178 experimental type, which made its maiden flight in August 1939.

110

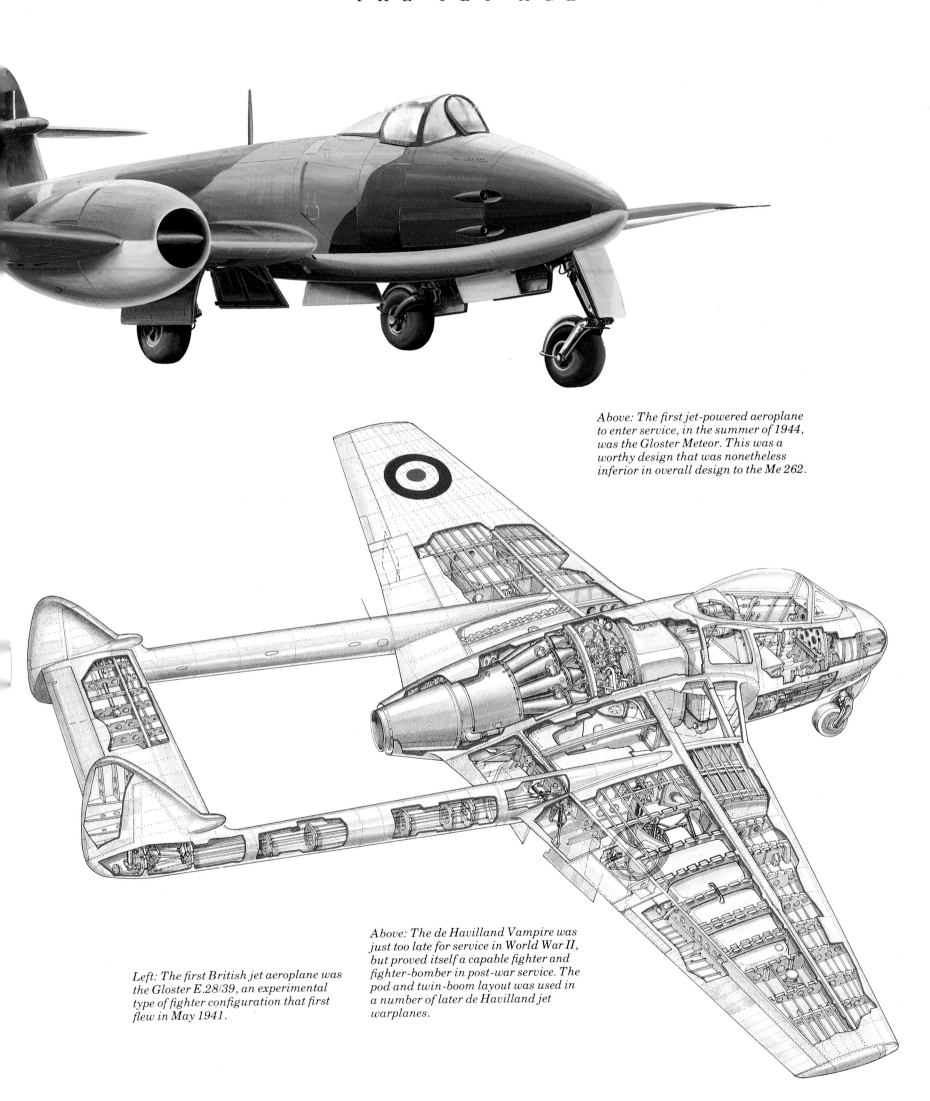

Above: The first jet-powered aeroplane to enter service, in the summer of 1944, was the Gloster Meteor. This was a worthy design that was nonetheless inferior in overall design to the Me 262.

Left: The first British jet aeroplane was the Gloster E.28/39, an experimental type of fighter configuration that first flew in May 1941.

Above: The de Havilland Vampire was just too late for service in World War II, but proved itself a capable fighter and fighter-bomber in post-war service. The pod and twin-boom layout was used in a number of later de Havilland jet warplanes.

From the end of World War II, the world had begun to repolarize politically and economically round the two superpowers that had emerged from the war and, as leaders of the Western and Eastern blocs, the USA and USSR pressed forward with the development of a new generation of weapons using indigenous efforts extensively upgraded by German research and, wherever possible, German designers.

This does not mean though, that there was a wholesale switch to turbojet power and its high subsonic performance. The jet engine was still an imperfect machine with poor reliability and stupendous fuel consumption.

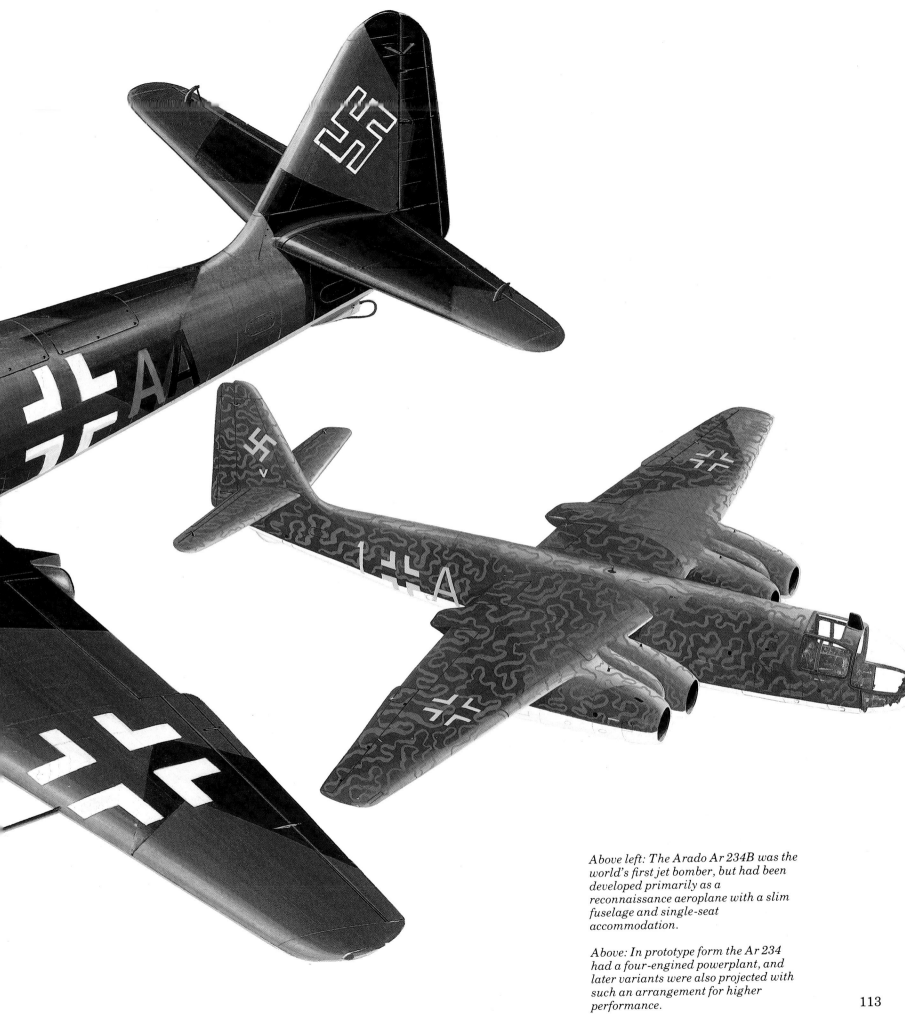

Above left: The Arado Ar 234B was the world's first jet bomber, but had been developed primarily as a reconnaissance aeroplane with a slim fuselage and single-seat accommodation.

Above: In prototype form the Ar 234 had a four-engined powerplant, and later variants were also projected with such an arrangement for higher performance.

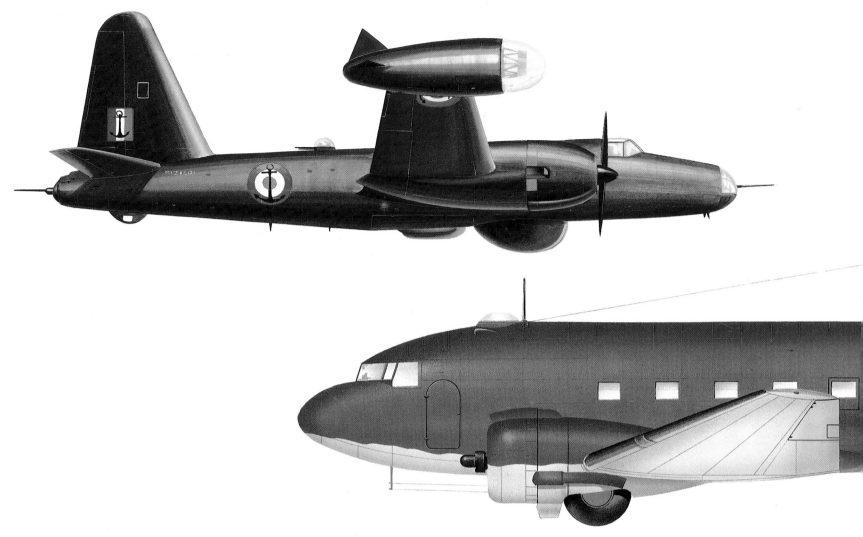

As such it was perhaps tolerable in high-performance combat aircraft, but not in planes designed for carrying substantial payloads over considerable range.

So the piston engine continued to serve into the early 1950s. Typical of the military aircraft that had seen service in World War II but still had development potential were the P-51 Mustang fighter and its long-range development, the P-82 Twin Mustang, which was essentially two Mustangs joined by a common centre section and tailplane, the F4U Corsair and its AU-7 ground-attack development, the Spitfire and its radical development the Spiteful, the Lancaster and its development the Lincoln, and the B-29 Superfortress and its up-engined development the B-50.

There were also a number of important planes developed to World War II specifications but which had been just too late for that war. The two classic aircraft of this type were the Convair B-36 superheavy bomber and the Douglas AD Skyraider carrierborne attack aeroplane. The B-36 had been planned as a definitive strategic bomber with hemispheric range capability, and matured as a vast machine with no fewer than six piston engines buried in the wings to drive pusher propellers. About half of the lower fuselage was devoted to bomb bays that could accommodate a maximum 86,000 lb of bombs, though with the advent of nuclear weapons its mission was generally planned round a very long-range sortie at high altitude with just a few massive bombs.

The pace of fighter development is indicated by the fact that this mighty bomber had to be fitted with four turbojets in two underwing pairs to boost

Far left: Developed during World War II as the Lockheed P2V, this exceptional maritime patroller became the western world's most important such aeroplane during the 1950s, and in the 1960s was redesignated the P-2 Neptune.

Below left and bottom: The Allies' most important transport and airborne forces' aeroplane in World War II and the period after it was the Douglas C-47 Skytrain, perhaps better known as the Dakota, the name bestowed first in British service.

performance. Additionally, development was undertaken of the McDonnell F-85 Goblin, a 'parasite' fighter to be carried internally by the B-36 and launched from an underfuselage trapeze to protect its parent over enemy territory before being recovered in a reversal of the launching procedure. The diminutive fighter had severe handling problems and was cancelled when it was appreciated that the B-36 would, in any case, have to be replaced by a more advanced jet-powered bomber.

The Skyraider was a large single-seat machine designed round a massive radial engine and external carriage for all its disposable armament. This made the Skyraider extremely versatile, while the high power-to-weight ratio combined with a capacious fuselage to make variants possible for roles as diverse as anti-submarine warfare and airborne early warning. The Skyraider seemed to have exhausted its variants and was apparently on the verge of obsolescence in the early 1960s. Then the USA entered the Vietnam War and the Skyraider was shown to be far from obsolete. The type served with the utmost distinction for the US Navy and US Air Force, the latter wishing that production had been greater when the extraordinary utility of the type was revealed. By comparison with most of its jet-powered successors, the Skyraider could carry just as large and diverse a warload, but its loiter time – the time it spent over its operational area – was greater, its response time to ground calls much faster, and its weapon-delivery accuracy superb.

But aircraft such as the Skyraider were the exception. From the end of World War II, the jet aeroplane came into its own as the premier warplane. First-generation machines had straight wings and were in essence piston-engined aircraft translated to jet power, as such offering only

115

relatively modest increases in performance over their forbears. Then the knock-on effect of German research began to make itself apparent as warplanes began to appear with the swept flying surfaces that delay the onset of the 'compressibility' and control problems associated with speeds approaching those of sound.

First in the field were the Americans and Soviets. Each flew a number of experimental aircraft in the period after World War II, and each

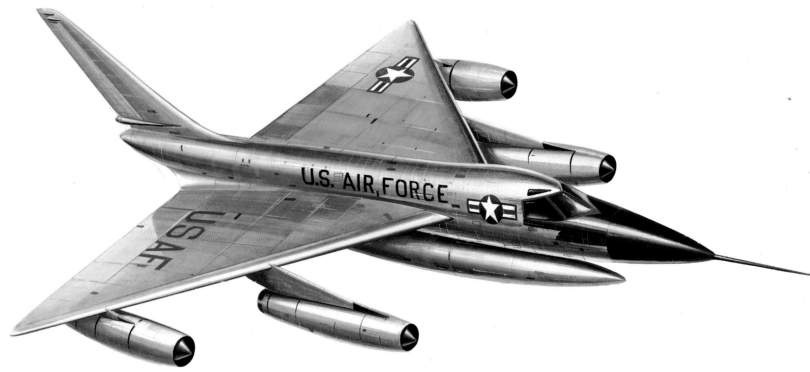

introduced a swept-wing fighter at about the same time. These were the North American F-86 Sabre and Mikoyan-Gurevich MiG-15, which proved far superior to any other fighters used in the Korean War (1950-1953) but were moderately well matched against each other. The American fighter was superior in equipment, speed and handling, while the Soviet fighter was superior in climb rate and, under certain conditions, turn rate. The Americans left the war with an 11:1 kill ratio between the Sabre and MiG-15, but this reflected the Americans' far superior training rather than outright superiority of their fighter.

Both these fighters were produced from the start with swept wings, but it is interesting to note that in service the American fighter was partnered by swept-wing derivatives of aircraft that had first entered service with straight wings – the Grumman F9F-6 Cougar and the Republic F-84F Thunderstreak which were based on the naval F9F Panther and air force F-84 Thunderjet fighter-bombers respectively. Both straight- and swept-wing versions remained in service for some time, but it was recognized even at the time that purpose-designed transonic fighters offered greater capabilities. The US Navy also devoted considerable effort to the development of tailless fighters, the two most successful being the Douglas F4D Skyray and Vought F7U Cutlass.

The Soviets moved forward with the MiG-17, a refined and more powerful derivative of the MiG-15 that was nevertheless firmly subsonic, while the Americans moved straight to supersonic types as the fighter mainstays of their air forces. The Europeans were some way behind the Americans and Soviets at this time with a number of single-seater fighters that were nevertheless worthy machines: the British fielded the Hawker Hunter and Supermarine Swift, the French the Dassault Mystére IV and the Swedes the Saab 29 Tunnen and Saab 32 Lansen.

There was also a parallel development of all-weather fighters, descendents of World War II night-fighters with air-intercept radar and firepower heavy enough to knock down large bombers. The period was marked by a slight shift in armament emphasis away from cannon, and a not inconsiderable number of these machines were fitted with large batteries of air-to-air rockets carried in retractable fuselage packs or in large pods at the wingtips. These rockets were mainly of 2.75-in calibre and the idea was to use radar for approach to the target whose general area would then be saturated with a salvo of unguided rockets. The limitations of such a tactic were readily apparent. Soon the world's first air-to-air missiles were carried by many of these fighters. Typical of the breed were the American Northrop F-89 Scorpion and Lockheed F-96 Starfire, the British Gloster Javelin, the Canadian Avro Canada CF-100 Canuck and the French SNCASO Vautour.

Meanwhile civil aviation was steadily closing the technical lead enjoyed by military aircraft. The spur to this improvement was the growing popularity and commercial importance of air travel. Post-war air services soon saw the disappearance of the flying boat. The war had effectively reduced the size of the world and witnessed the building of airfields in many remote areas. These airfields were generally adequate for the ex-military machines that flooded onto the civil market. Britain and France made efforts to break back into this lucrative business, but it was the Americans who capitalized on maintenance, improvement and finally replacement of the aircraft they had built in the first place.

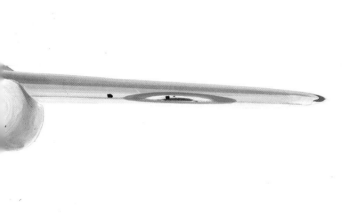

Left: The USSR's first completely effective jet fighter was the Mikoyan-Gurevich MiG-15, rival to the North American F-86 Sabre in the skies over Korea in the early 1950s.

Left: As soon as the technology permitted, the Americans moved forward to the supersonic strategic bomber in the Convair B-58 Hustler. This was an extraordinary achievement in the technical sense. Over the target the B-58 was designed to jettison its large underfuselage pod, which accommodated the weapon load and fuel for the outward leg of the mission.

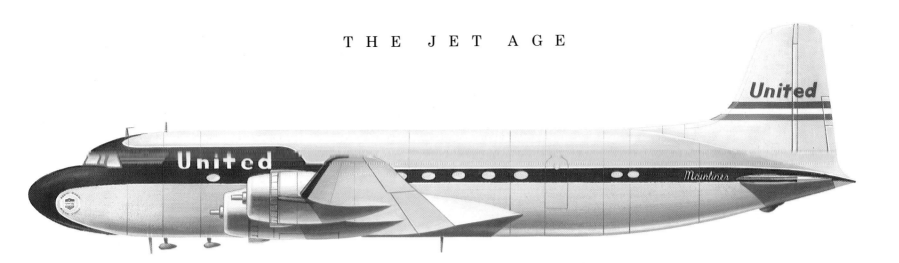

During the late 1940s and early 1950s a large number of piston-engine airliners appeared, and this selection shows a number of different configurations and sizes. From top to bottom on the left are the Short Sandringham (a development of the wartime Sunderland maritime patroller), the Lockheed L-1049 Super Constellation, the Curtiss Commando and the Convair CV-340. From top to bottom on the right are the Douglas DC-4, the de Havilland Heron and the Ilyushin Il-14.

The C-47 soldiered on in vast numbers through the 1940s, 1950s and 1960s, only declining in numbers to significant degree in the 1970s. This made it difficult for any other aircraft to compete in this market, as witness the failure of the Martin 4-0-4 and the comparatively modest success of the higher-performance Convair CV-240, 340 and 440 series. Where air transport boomed, however, was in medium and long-range operations, and here the Americans truly dominated with the output of the Boeing, Douglas and Lockheed companies.

Boeing was the least successful of the three with its bluff-nosed Model 377 Stratocruiser, the civil equivalent of the C-97 Stratofreighter military transport. The Stratocruiser failed to secure large production contracts, but proved immensely popular with passengers for its spacious twin-deck accommodation and the full pressurization that allowed it to cruise comfortably above the weather. Douglas moved forward from its wartime DC-4 (C-54 Skymaster) with the pressurized DC-6 for transcontinental routes and the more powerful, heavier DC-7 for intercontinental routes.

However it was Lockheed to whom the honour fell of producing the world's greatest piston-engined airliner series – the Constellation. This had entered limited military service in World War II when the initial L-049 variant was taken into military service as the C-69. But though the type was procured for the military in many of its later variants – and has the distinction of being the basis for the world's first effective long-range airborne early warning aeroplane – the Constellation is best remembered as a civil transport. Powered by successively more potent variants of the great Wright R-3350 Cyclone radial, the Constellation entered service in its first wholly civil version as the L-649 and long-range L-749 versions. The L-1049 Super Constellation was a refined and lengthened version, and the ultimate version of the series was the L-1649 Starliner, which must go down in history as the most elegant piston-engined airliner ever built.

As with military aircraft, the death-knell of the piston-engined airliner was spelled by the turbojet. Here it was the British who led the way with the remarkable de Havilland Comet. This first flew with de Havilland Ghost engines as a medium-range aeroplane designed for the carriage of mail and a modest number of passengers. It was soon appreciated, however, that the centrifugal-flow Ghost had inferior operating economics to the rapidly developing axial-flow engines which were becoming available. In the Comet 2 the switch was made to Rolls-Royce Avon

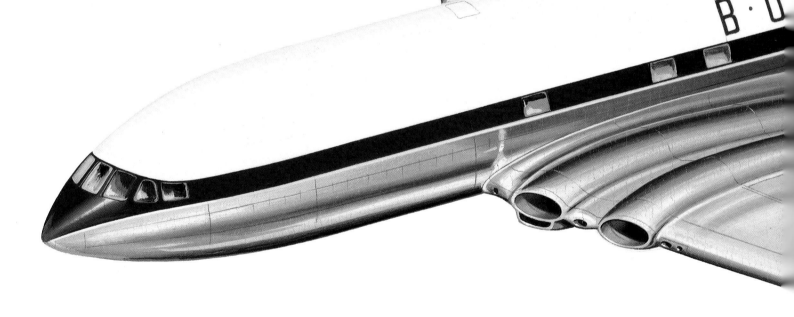

engines – four of these became the definitive powerplant. It appeared that Britain might gain a decisive lead in the development of jet airliners, but then the whole Comet airliner programme was jeopardized by the loss of two aircraft over the Mediterranean in 1954. The wrecks were partially recovered and the cause determined to be metal fatigue in the corners of the square-cut windows, leading to explosive decompression of the cabin. The solution – the development of a safer round-windowed fuselage – took time. This allowed the Americans to catch up and overtake before the Comet 4 was ready for service.

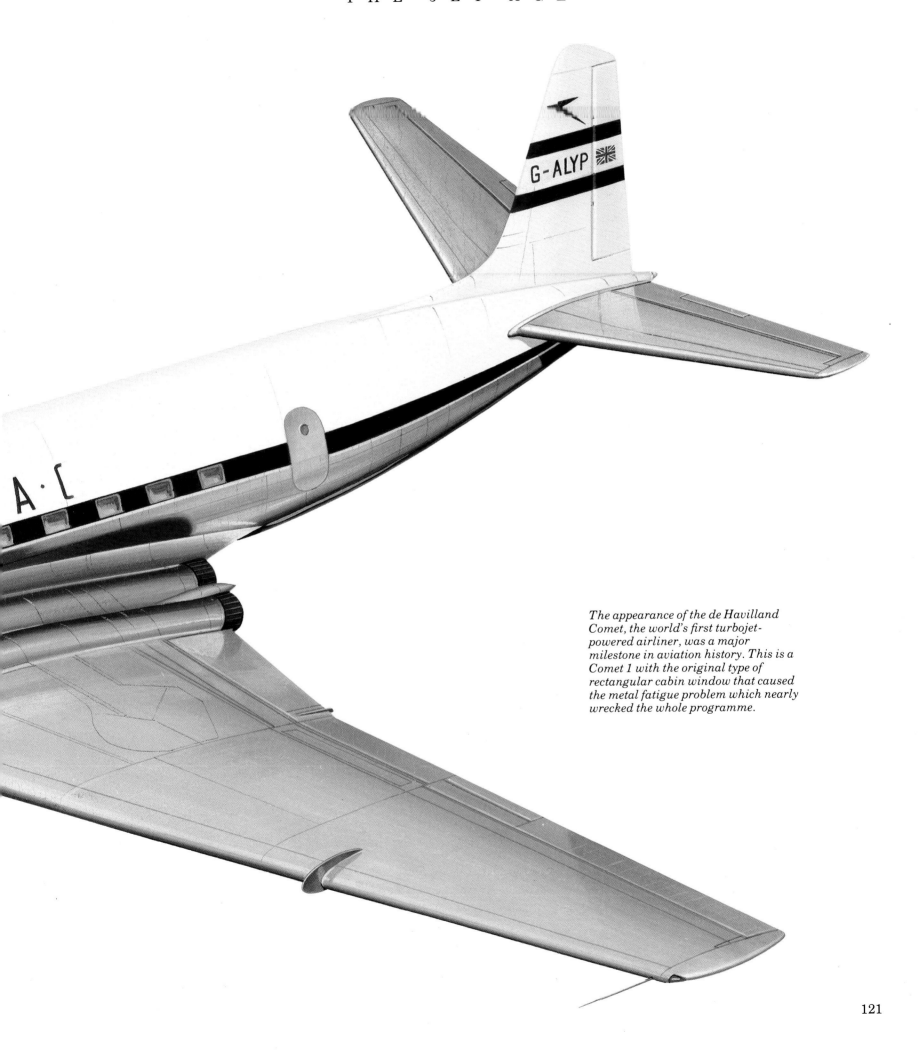

The appearance of the de Havilland Comet, the world's first turbojet-powered airliner, was a major milestone in aviation history. This is a Comet 1 with the original type of rectangular cabin window that caused the metal fatigue problem which nearly wrecked the whole programme.

The aircraft that overtook the Comet were the Boeing Model 707, the Convair CV-880 and the Douglas DC-8. The CV-880 was a commercial failure. Its designers mistakenly thought it could beat the earlier 707 and DC-8 by offering smaller capacity but significantly higher speed. With the failure of the CV-880 and its CV-990 Coronado derivative, Convair – and its successor General Dynamics – pulled out of airliner manufacture. This

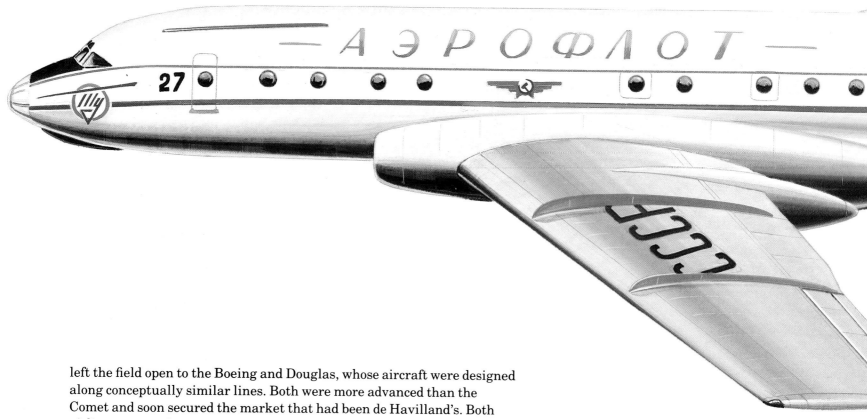

left the field open to the Boeing and Douglas, whose aircraft were designed along conceptually similar lines. Both were more advanced than the Comet and soon secured the market that had been de Havilland's. Both airliners entered service in the late 1950s, but while Douglas was content to offer a single fuselage in several weight and engine options, Boeing was more ambitious and offered different fuselage lengths as well. The result was that while both aircraft were commercially successful, the 707 sold better and must be credited with the opening of modern air transport as a mass market. Some measure of the 707's success may be gauged from the fact that, in the UK, the Vickers VC10 was developed as a competitor with a larger wing and lower landing speed – the British were convinced that many countries would be unwilling, or not financially able, to expand their airport runway lengths to cater for the American aircraft with their higher landing speeds and longer runway requirements. The VC10 was a technical success but a commercial flop. Every major – and most minor – airports scrambled to expand their runways to meet the requirements of the Model 707 and DC-8.

The Soviets were, in fact, the second nation into the turbojet field with the Tupolev Tu-104, an airliner development of the Tu-16 medium strategic bomber. And the French were not far behind the first three with the SNCASE Caravelle, the world's first short/medium-range jet airliner with the nose of the Comet and the pioneering feature of twin turbojets attached to the sides of the rear fuselage to leave the wing uncluttered.

Above: The Tupolev Tu-104 was the world's second jetliner to enter service, and was in essence the civil counterpart to the Tu-16 twin-jet bomber.

There were also turboprop-powered airliners, offering the advantages of a turbine engine with its smooth running and its mechanical lack of complexity with the aerodynamic and fuel advantages of the propeller at modest airspeeds. The world's first successful turboprop airliner was the British Vickers Viscount. Another country swift to enter this short-range race was the Netherlands with the Fokker F.27 Friendship, which was also built in the USA as the Fairchild F-27 and developed further as the Fairchild FH-227. Medium-range turboprop airliners included the Bristol Britannia and Lockheed L-188 Electra, while in the long-range stakes there was a development of the Britannia and, from the USSR, the extraordinary Tupolev Tu-114, the civil derivative of the swept-wing Tu-95 bomber with four huge turboprops each driving a contra-rotating propeller unit.

Below: The Tupolev Tu-114 was the civil counterpart to the Tu-95 strategic bomber, with well swept flying surfaces and four massively powerful turboprops each driving a contra-rotating propeller unit. The result was very high performance over long ranges.

Allied technologically to these civil airliners were the new generation of military transports. Lockheed led the way with the superb C-130 Hercules that set the pattern for all modern military transports with its high wing and main landing gear units in external blisters, leaving the fuselage clear

for the load, which is loaded through a powered rear ramp/door arrangement that allows vehicle to be driven into the hold. This arrangement also permits simple paradropping. The Soviet equivalent to the Hercules is the Antonov An-12. Another notable transport of the period is the twin-turboprop Transall C.160 designed and produced jointly by France and West Germany.

In the bomber, too, the jet engine and swept wing had their parts to play. There had been a number of first-generation jet bombers with straight wings, most notably the English Electric Canberra, the Soviet Ilyushin Il-28 and the North American B-45 Tornado. But these were rapidly overhauled by advanced swept-wing machines. First off the mark was the Boeing B-47 Stratojet, an extraordinarily ambitious medium strategic bomber with six turbojets in underwing pods, highly swept flying surfaces and a slender fuselage supported on tandem main landing gear units balanced by underwing outrigger units. The same basic concept was followed for the Boeing B-52 Stratofortress, successor to the B-36 and still, numerically, the most important bomber operated by the USA. This eight-engined machine offered greater range and payload than the B-47, especially when used with the USA's large inflight-refuelling tanker fleet.

The USA's first effective tanker was the KC-97 version of the C-97 Stratofreighter, useful when America's strategic bomber force was equipped with the piston-engined B-36 and B-50. But even with its performance boosted by two underwing turbojets, the KC-97 lacked the performance to support the B-47 and B-52, and was replaced by the legendary Boeing KC-135 Stratotanker. This was the basic aeroplane from which the 707 was derived, the company having recovered much of its massive investment in design and production tooling with the large orders placed by the US Air Force for the tanker variant.

The USSR did not at the time follow this route into mid-air refuelling and had to rely on the medium-range Tu-16 and two prodigious long-range types, the Myasishchyev M-4 and the Tupolev Tu-95. Neither of these possessed the range for a sustained strategic offensive against the USA, but each was in its own way a remarkable achievement – the M-4 with its quartet of powerful turbojets buried in the wing roots and the Tu-95 with its four turboprops. Both aircraft remain in service, albeit mainly in other roles.

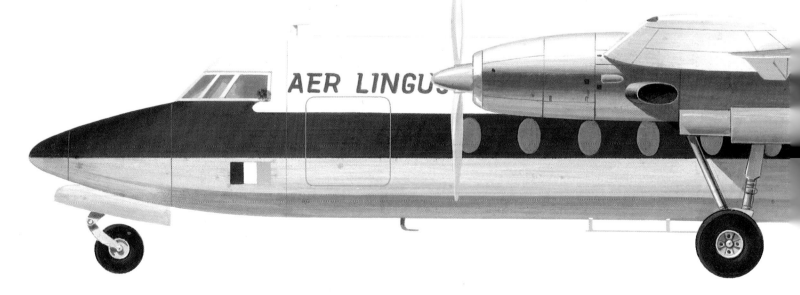

Above: The Vickers Vanguard was intended to succeed the pioneering Vickers Viscount as a short/medium-range turboprop airliner, but failed to emulate the success of its predecessor.

Below: One of the most successful twin-turboprop airliners has been the Fokker F.27 Friendship, which entered service in the late 1950s and, in its radically updated F50 form, remains in production.

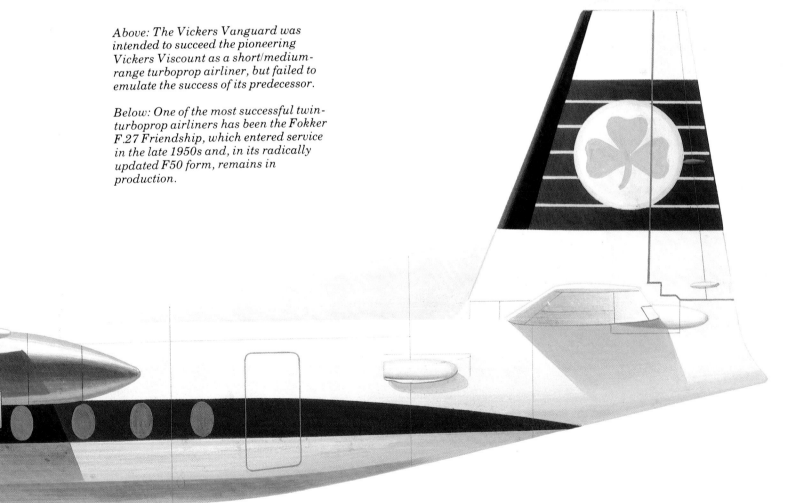

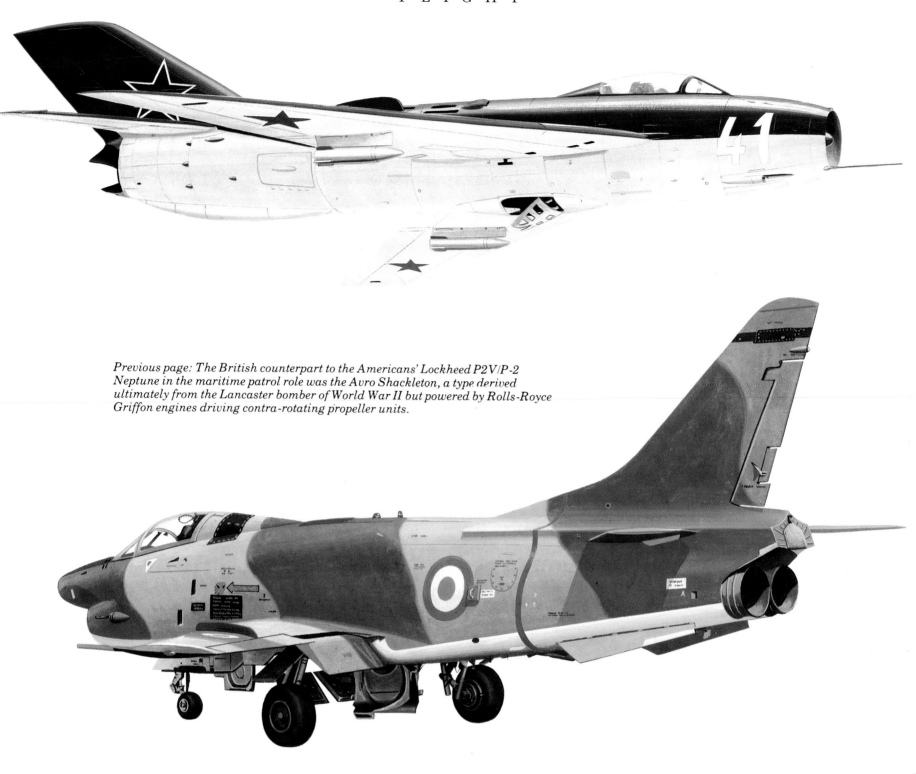

Previous page: The British counterpart to the Americans' Lockheed P2V/P-2 Neptune in the maritime patrol role was the Avro Shackleton, a type derived ultimately from the Lancaster bomber of World War II but powered by Rolls-Royce Griffon engines driving contra-rotating propeller units.

The only other nation with a strategic bombing requirement in this period was the UK, which squandered enormous potential advantages in putting into production no fewer than three of its so-called 'V-bombers'. The Vickers Valiant was a low-risk development of unexceptional capabilities, the Avro Vulcan was a large delta-winged aeroplane with its useful load and range, and the Handley Page Victor was an advanced design of good load and range. The Vulcan and Victor survived into the 1980s, the former securing the distinction of having made the longest bomber raids ever recorded when attacking Stanley Airport in the Falkland Islands from Ascension Island in 1982. From the late 1960s, the Victor form was successively modified for the tanker role as the Valiant tankers were retired as a result of metal fatigue.

From the middle of the 1950s technological developments made possible the first generation of transonic and genuinely supersonic military aircraft as epitomized by these machines. Clockwise from top left these are the Mikoyan-Gurevich MiG-19 from the USSR, the Republic F-84F Thunderjet (a development of the straight-winged Thunderstreak) from the USA, the Republic XF-91 prototype with inversely tapered wing and a mixed turbojet/rocket powerplant, and the Aeritalia (Fiat) G91Y from Italy.

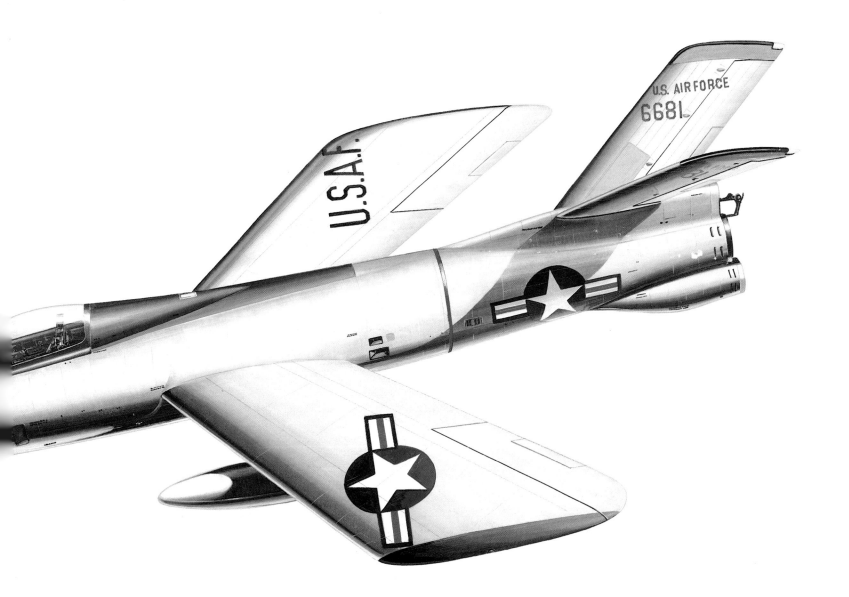

CHAPTER SEVEN: THE SOUND BARRIER

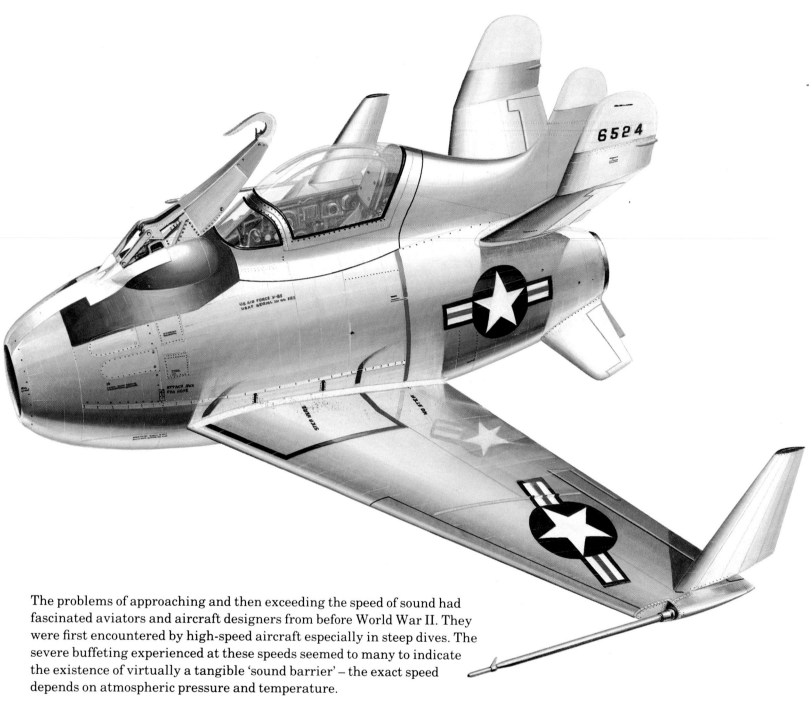

The problems of approaching and then exceeding the speed of sound had fascinated aviators and aircraft designers from before World War II. They were first encountered by high-speed aircraft especially in steep dives. The severe buffeting experienced at these speeds seemed to many to indicate the existence of virtually a tangible 'sound barrier' – the exact speed depends on atmospheric pressure and temperature.

Several experimental aircraft were lost because of control failure or buffet-induced structural failure at transonic speed. But in 1947 'Chuck' Yeager at the controls of the rocket-powered Bell X-1 at last pushed past Mach 1, the local speed of sound. Growing familiarity with the transonic region produced the data on which the designers could evolve the solution to the problems of 'breaking the sound barrier', and by the early 1950s experimental aircraft were pushing well past Mach 1 and opening the possibility of supersonic speed.

Left: The McDonnell XF-85 Goblin was designed for carriage in the bomb bay of the Convair B-36 strategic bomber, but proved to have impossible handling characteristics.

Above: The English Electric Lighting was the only supersonic warplane of wholly British design to enter service.

Below: The Dassault Mirage III is an elegant delta-winged design offering Mach 2 performance.

Bottom: The Sukhoi Su-15 is a Mach 2+ interceptor designed for operation under strict ground control as part of the USSR's air-defence system.

The difficulty lay in translating this research capability into a warplane that could be mass produced and then operated supersonically as a matter of course without the special maintenance and other equipment associated with research programmes. It was the Americans and the Soviets who pushed the process along fastest in their efforts each to secure a military advantage over the other in the dire opening days of the Cold War. The result was the virtually simultaneous service debut of the world's first two supersonic fighters, the single-engined North American F-100 Super Sabre and the twin-engined Mikoyan-Gurevich MiG-19. The aircraft were of basically similar configuration with highly swept flying surfaces and a nose inlet for engine air. But while the American machine was notable for its high wing loading and capability for considerable external stores, the MiG-19 was of considerably lower wing loading, giving it far superior agility.

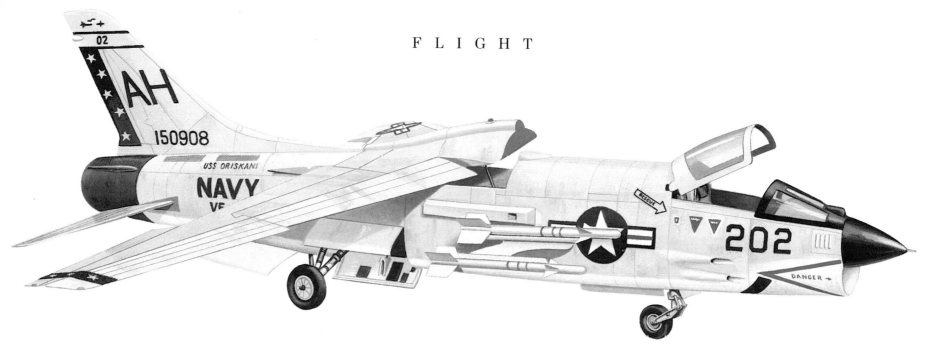

The Americans thought that agility was an obsolete factor: the object of supersonic performance, after all, was to close the range on a target as rapidly as possible and then destroy it with missiles or failing that, cannon fire. The Soviets were more confident of the benefits of cannon fire over early guided missiles and placed a premium on manoeuvrability as a means of avoiding the enemy's first pass and then closing on him to effective cannon range. There is no doubt, as hindsight has revealed, that the Soviets were right. The F-100 is no longer in service, while the MiG-19 remains in service in its original Soviet form, and in the form of the Shenyang J-6 produced in China. The fallacy of the American concept first began to come clear in the Vietnam War, where the MiG-19s flown by North Vietnamese pilots often managed to evade American missiles and close with the US tactical aircraft, forcing them to manoeuvre and lose speed, engaging them in the type of turning fight where the agility of the communist fighters was superior to that of the US machines.

But this was not foreseen by the designers of the USA and, later, Europe. Supersonic flight capability became a goal almost in its own right. From this it was a natural progression to Mach 2 using increasingly powerful engines with fuel-guzzling afterburners and a number of aerodynamic features such as area-ruled fuselages. Mach 2.25 became the practical

Above: The Vough F-8 Crusader carrierborne fighter was designed as the F8U and featured a variable-incidence wing that allowed low-speed landings with the fuselage level so that the pilot could see the flightdeck properly.

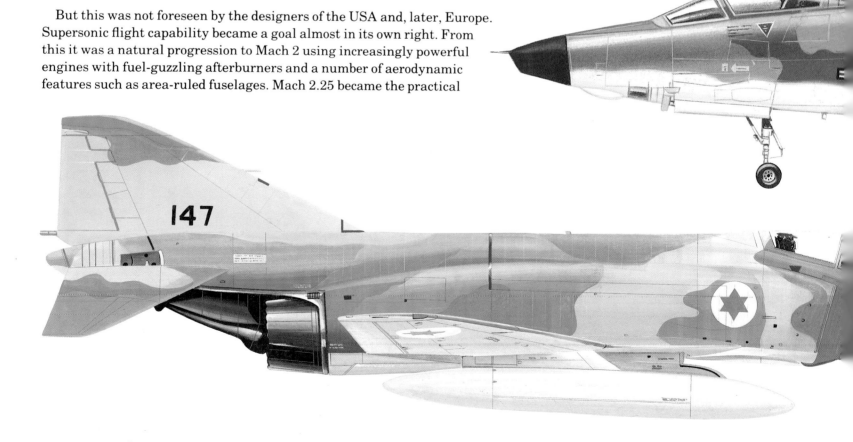

maximum for combat aircraft because of the limitations imposed by a primary structure of aluminium alloy. Above this speed it begins to lose its strength as a result of aerodynamic heating.

Other US Air Force fighters capable of speeds above Mach 1 were the McDonnell F-101 Voodoo long-range all-weather fighter and the Convair F-102 Delta Dagger interceptor fighter. The former was planned as a penetration fighter but matured as a tactical and air-defence machine. The latter was planned as a highly supersonic interception weapon system integrated into the SAGE (Semi-Automatic Ground Environment) system of ground-based radars and control systems to co-ordinate the whole of the North American air defence, but matured as a modestly supersonic type with good weapon capability. The US Navy also went for Mach 1+ performance, proceeding via the interim Grumman F11F Tiger to the much underestimated Vought F8U Crusader. This latter had performance superior to that of the Super Sabre, yet could operate from aircraft-carrier decks without undue difficulty because of its unique variable-incidence wings. These were pivoted around the rear spar so that, as the Crusader approached its carrier, the wings' angle of incidence could be increased while the fuselage was kept in the level, providing the pilot with the optimum field of vision.

Below: The McDonnell F-101 Voodoo was designed as a long-range escort fighter, but after a chequered early career entered service as an interceptor and reconnaissance type.

Bottom: The finest warplane of the 1960s was the McDonnell (later McDonnell Douglas) F-4 Phantom II. This entered service as a carrierborne fighter, but was soon accepted as a land-based type and is seen here in the form of the definitive F-4E variant with a multi-barrel cannon built into the lower nose.

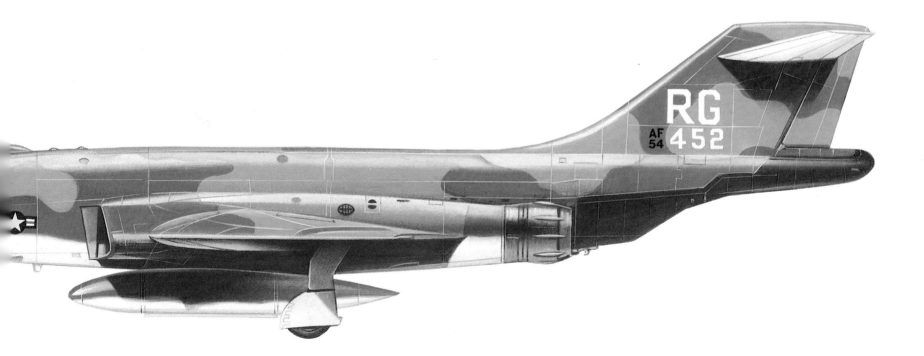

The only European country to follow the American lead into Mach 1 performance was France, whose Dassault Super Mystère was a radical development of the transonic Mystère IV. At this time, Europe was also concerned with lightweight fighters and fighter-bombers: the tactical scenario envisaged at the time for a third world war supposed that the Soviets would target all major European air bases for attack. The hope was that such lightweight types could operate from undamaged runway sections between craters or roads or, as a last resort, fields. Several interesting designs resulted, the most notable being the Fiat G91 from Italy that was produced in modest numbers for its parent country and for West Germany. Another lightweight was the Dassault Etendard, which became the parent of the Etendard IVM naval fighter.

133

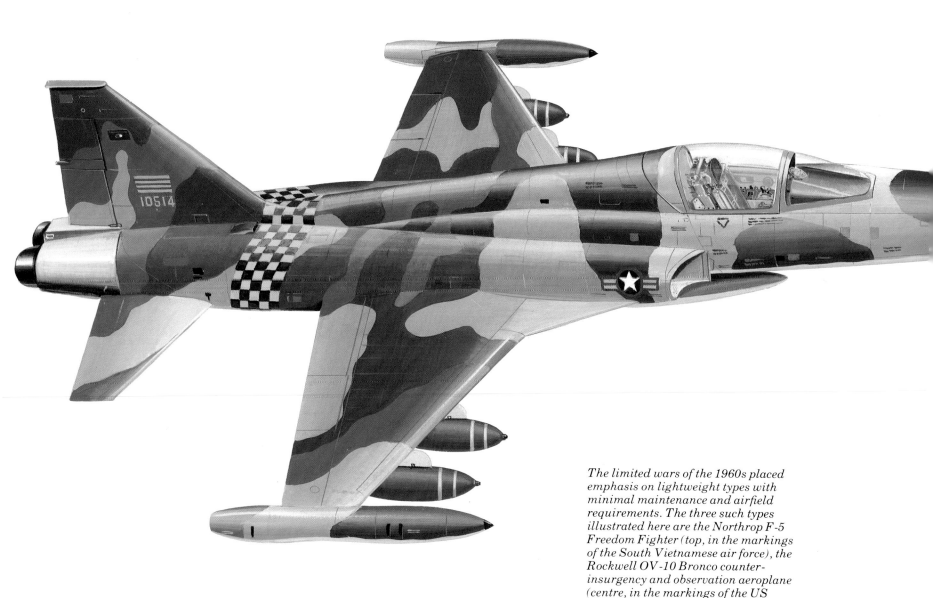

The limited wars of the 1960s placed emphasis on lightweight types with minimal maintenance and airfield requirements. The three such types illustrated here are the Northrop F-5 Freedom Fighter (top, in the markings of the South Vietnamese air force), the Rockwell OV-10 Bronco counter-insurgency and observation aeroplane (centre, in the markings of the US Marine Corps) and the Cessna A-37 Dragonfly light attack aeroplane (bottom, in South Vietnamese markings).

In the UK there was increasing concern about the development, production and operating cost of the American type of heavyweight fighter, and this was reflected in the development of the diminutive but capable Folland Gnat. This fighter was procured in small numbers by India, which also built the Gnat under licence as the Ajeet, and Finland, while the Royal Air Force took the Gnat as an advanced trainer. British naval aviation was more concerned with overall capabilities than outright supersonic performance. As a result such excellent machines as the de Havilland Sea Vixen all-weather fighter and the Supermarine Scimitar strike fighter, both capable of high subsonic performance, were produced.

The US Navy also felt that there was scope for subsonic attack aircraft to operate beside its supersonic fighters and looked for a jet-powered successor to the Skyraider. The result was the classic Douglas A4D Skyhawk, a small machine that weighed in at about half of the US Navy's upper limit for such a plane, but fully filled the operational requirement in performance and warload. The Skyraider proved enormously successful in service, later variants having a different and more powerful engine, additional electronics, and a larger and more varied warload. So successful

has the Skyhawk been that many were later supplied to smaller countries for use in land- and carrier-based roles, and many still survive to the present. Moreover, such are the capabilities of the type that there is a small but thriving industry devoted to the upgrade of surviving aircraft with modern radar and other electronics, provision for more advanced weapons and even, in some cases, turbofan engines for better performance with reduced fuel consumption.

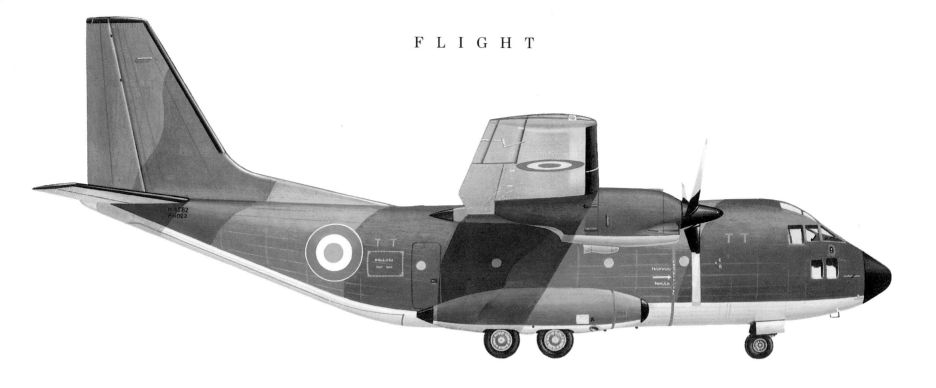

The A4D was partnered by the altogether larger Douglas A3D Skywarrior, which retains the distinction of having been the heaviest aeroplane to have operated regularly from a carrier deck. This was planned as the US Navy's delivery platform for strategic nuclear weapons. It was a long-range aircraft with large internal weapons bay. But the navy lost its strategic nuclear tasking not long after the type entered service and Skywarriors were used for electronic countermeasures and as inflight-refuelling tankers. The US Air Force operated a land-based variant, the B-66 Destroyer.

Increasingly, though, there was emphasis on Mach 2+ performance with advanced radar and a primary armament of missiles. The US Air Force put into production the Lockheed F-104 Starfighter, the Republic F-105 Thunderchief and the Convair F-106 Delta Dart. The Starfighter was planned as a dedicated interceptor with a phenomenal turn of climb and speed, and has been aptly likened to a manned missile because of its long fuselage, stretching from a pointed probe to a substantial T-tail, combined with tiny straight wings. The F-105 was an altogether more massive aeroplane planned for a tactical strike role with conventional or nuclear weapons. The Delta Dart was what the generally similar Delta Dagger had failed to be, namely a potent missile-armed interceptor with Mach 2 performance.

The USSR followed along broadly the same path, albeit with modifications demanded by a nation which has long emphasized tactical air support for the ground forces. Together with the continued requirement for agility, this has produced such notable aircraft as the Mikoyan-Gurevich MiG-21 clear-weather interceptor with a useful ground-attack capability in its later variants, the Sukhoi Su-7 ground-attack fighter, the Sukhoi Su-11 and Su-15 all-weather interceptors, the Tupolev Tu-28 long-range all-weather interceptor and the Yakovlev Yak-28 all-weather fighter.

The European experience was derived basically from that of the Americans, and three nations produced genuine Mach 2 fighters. These

Stemming ultimately from a NATO requirement for a vertical take-off tactical transport, the Aeritalia G222 is a conventional tactical airlifter.

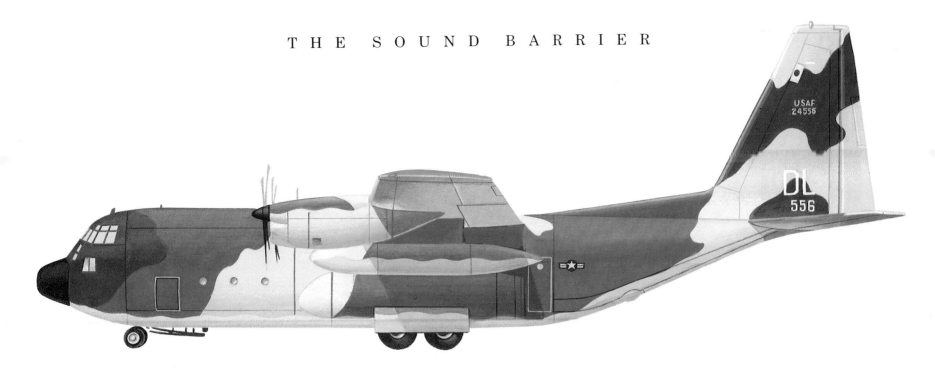

Above: The aeroplane that pioneered the modern configuration of military transports (multi-wheel landing gear, high wing and upswept tail over a rear ramp/door) is the Lockheed C-130 Hercules.

Below: An older transport designed in the aftermath of World War II, was the piston-engined Handley Page Hastings.

countries were France with the Dassault Mirage III delta-wing multi-role fighter and its Mirage 5 clear-weather ground-attack fighter derivative, Sweden with its impressive Saab 35 Draken double-delta interceptor and attack aeroplane, and the UK with its aggressive-looking English Electric Lightning interceptor which only went out of service in 1988. The Mirage III and 5 family became a world best seller and is still an important combat type in several smaller air forces. The Saab 35 Draken is still a valuable asset with four operators, but the British fighter was characterized by two common failings of British interceptors, namely short range and light armament.

Without a shadow of a doubt, however, the greatest military aeroplane of the initial Mach 2 generation was the Phantom II first known as the McDonnell F4H and now as the McDonnell Douglas F-4. The plane was originally planned as a carrierborne attack aeroplane, but while on the drawing boards was modified as a two-seat fleet defence fighter carrying powerful radar and an all-missile armament. It entered service as fighter with an exceptional secondary attack capability and was soon developed into a tactical reconnaissance variant for the US Marine Corps. So capable were these aircraft that the US Air Force also ordered equivalents. This started a programme that saw the construction of more than 5,000 Phantoms for US and widespread export service. The Phantom became the

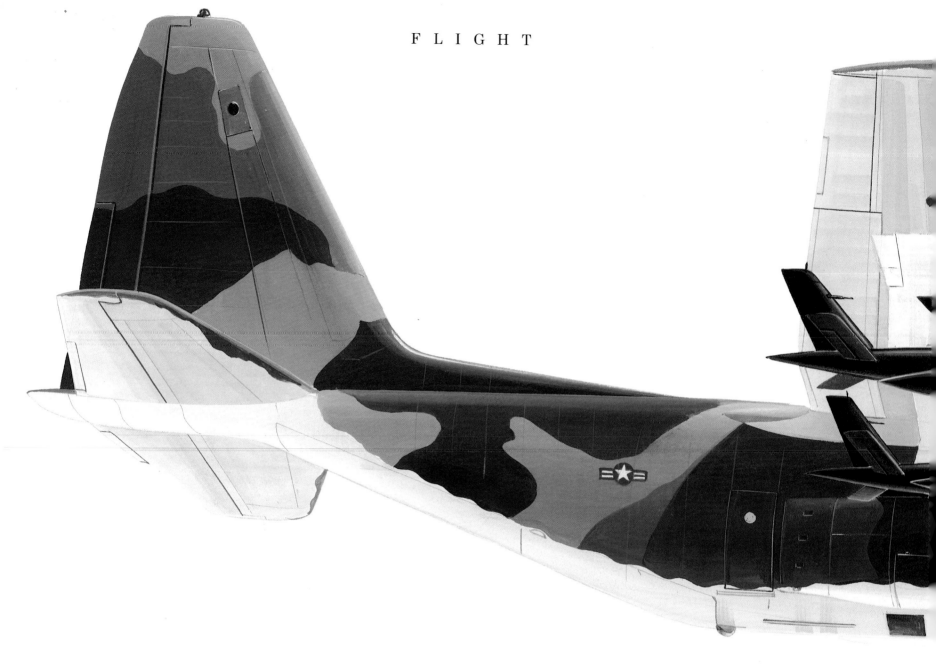

US workhorse of the air campaign in the Vietnam War, where it was
shown to have failings, principally in armament and manoeuvrability. The
lack of cannon armament was remedied in the short term by the carriage
of an underfuselage cannon pod, but while this installation was adequate
for ground-attack work it vibrated too much for accurate shooting in
air-combat. The US Air Force's F-4E variant introduced an internal
cannon of the M61 Vulcan rotary type, with six barrels turning round a
common axis like a Gatling gun to provide the required volume of fire.
Agility was improved by modifications to the outer wings and tailplane,
but in so large a beast as the Phantom these improvements were
necessarily palliatives rather than a complete cure. The Phantom is now
past its prime, but is still so important in numerical terms that existing
aircraft are being steadily upgraded in a number of countries. Israel has
undertaken the most extensive effort to produce the completely updated
Phantom 2000. The basic capabilities of the type have also prompted the
US Air Force to modify a substantial number as F-4G 'Wild Weasel'
aircraft with the sensors to detect enemy radars and the computerized
control system to analyse their type and fire and appropriately cued
missile to take them out.

Mach 2 performance was also thought desirable for bombers and heavy
attack aircraft in the 1950s, and this perception spurred development of
some of the most ambitious aircraft in aviation history. The US effort was

The Lockheed C-130 Hercules was designed as a tactical transport, but in a long development and production career has been evolved into a host of other roles including, as here, the launch (and sometimes the aerial recovery) of drones and remotely piloted vehicles.

headed by Convair (in both its original and later General Dynamics forms) and North American (again in its original and later Rockwell forms). Convair was responsible for the B-58 Hustler medium strategic bomber, a formidable delta-winged plane with four large turbojets pod-mounted below the wing and a massive underfuselage pod that contained, in addition to its nuclear payload, the fuel for the outward leg of the attack: the pod was jettisoned over the target allowing the lightened and drag-reduced Hustler to make good its escape. But as the Hustler began to enter service it was becoming clear that the day of the high-altitude bomber was gone. Surface-to-air missiles were now sufficiently accurate and reliable to require penetration of enemy airspace below the radar horizon.

Older bombers were adapted to carry stand-off missiles rather than free-fall weapons. This meant that the aeroplane had no reason to overfly heavily defended major targets. It also helped to restore some of attack radius lost by the need to operate at lower level with consequently increased fuel consumption. The B-52 was modified for this role, and so too were the British V-bombers, but what was required was a new type of bomber designed aerodynamically and structually for the thicker and more turbulent air encountered at low altitude.

139

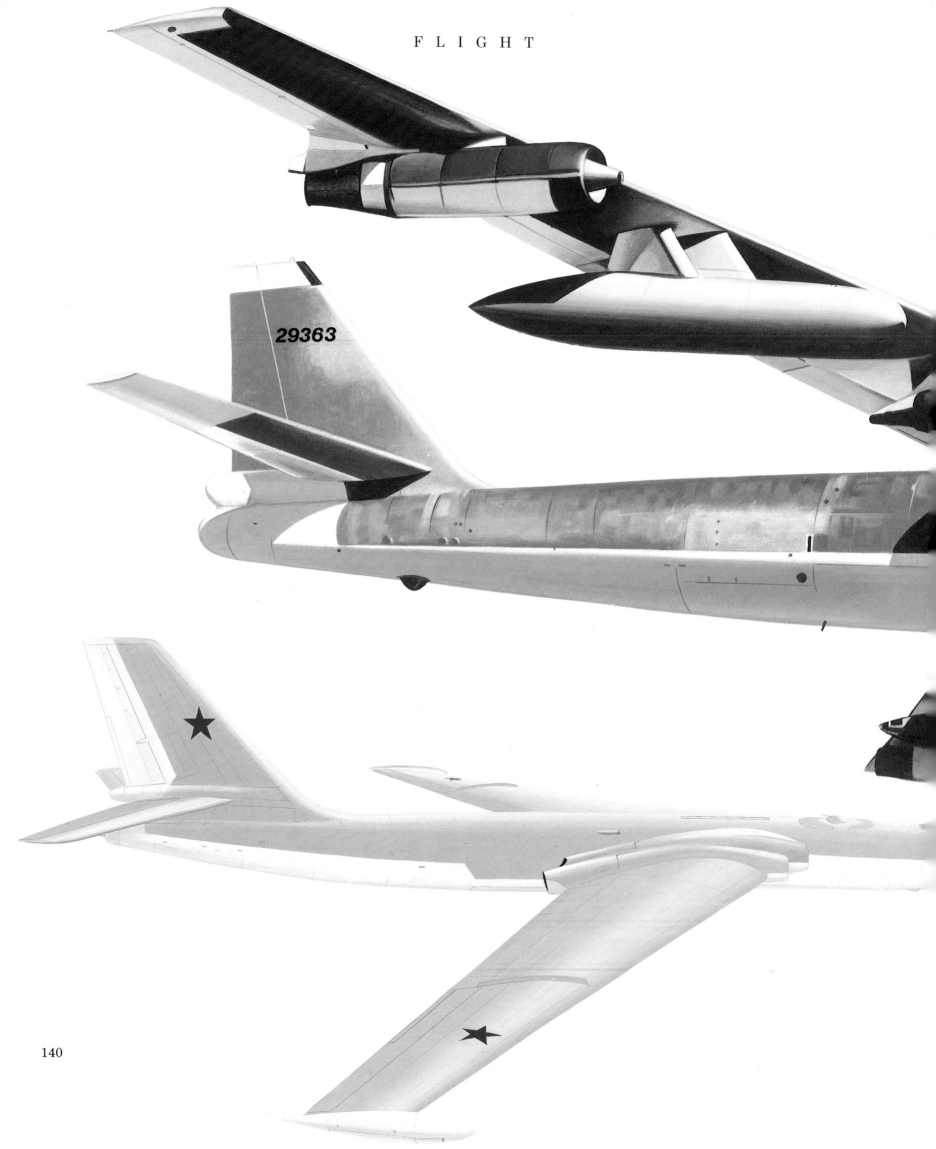

29363

sweep position for maximum lift and controllability at take-off, cruising

Below: The Boeing B-47 Stratojet was an enormous technical achievement, and provided the US Air Force's Strategic Air Command with its highest performance strategic bomber until the advent of the same company's B-52 Stratofortress in the mid 1950s.

Left: On the other side of the Iron Curtain, the Myasishchyev M-4 was a considerably larger and heavier aeroplane than the B-47, but an equal technological achievement.

General Dynamics was responsible for the F-111, often called the 'Aardvark' and the world's first variable-geometry – 'swing-wing' – aeroplane. These planes can move their wings between the minimum-sweep position for maximum lift and controllability at take-off, cruising flight and landing, and the maximum-sweep position for minimum drag when high-speed flight is required. The F-111 has been produced in several variants including the FB-111 medium strategic bomber, mostly optimized for the long-range attack of key points deep in the enemy rear. The type was at first hampered by electronic limitations, but has matured as one of the West's vital aircraft able to operate in all weathers and at very low altitudes for attacks on key installations and communications chokepoints in the enemy's rear areas.

North American produced for the US Navy the impressive A-5 Vigilante, a Mach 2 attack bomber with its nuclear payload and outward-leg fuel tanks in a ventral tunnel for rearward ejection over the target. Again the demise of high-altitude operating desirability put paid to

the type in its intended role soon after service entry, and the Vigilante was therefore revised for recoonnaissance. As Rockwell, North American also developed the ultimate high-altitude bomber, the B-70 Valkyrie. This was a Mach 3 machine of huge size with six engines in tunnels under the main delta wing, mounted at the rear of this canard design. The Valkyrie reached prototype form, but was then seen to be operationally obsolete and cancelled.

The USSR also produced a number of experimental bombers of the supersonic high-altitude type, but of these the only one to enter limited production was the Tupolev Tu-22, a medium-range type that clearly possessed a number of limitations that severely curtailed production plans. France produced a medium-range type in the Dassault Mirage IV, essentially a scaled-up version of the Mirage III with twin engines, and the UK reached prototype form with the truly exceptional BAC TSR-2, a low-level tactical strike and reconnaissance aeroplane of ambitious design whose development problems were being eradicated steadily when it was cancelled for wholly partisan political reasons.

The TSR-2 was to have been replaced by a version of the F-111, but this failed to materialize in the planned timeframe and was ultimately cancelled by the British government. A sort of successor was then found in the SEPECAT Jaguar, a collaborative Anglo-French aeroplane designed as a modestly supersonic advanced trainer but ultimately found to possess the low-level range, payload and handling characteristics that made it an ideal candidate for development as an attack and strike aeroplane. It has been used mainly by the British and French, the former fielding a more powerful version with considerably more sophisticated electronics than the latter. Significant numbers were also produced for export in upgraded forms that include maritime search radar in the case of at least some Indian machines.

Left: The first variable-geometry aeroplane to enter service was the General Dynamics F-111 interdictor, seen here in the form of an F-111A, the initial production variant.

142

Above: Developed slightly later, the Mikoyan-Gurevich MiG-23 fighter uses variable-geometry wings to secure a combination of good field performance with the wings in minimum-sweep position and high performance with the wings in maximum-sweep position.

Below: The Douglas B-66 Destroyer was a land-based attack bomber derived from the US Navy's A3D Skywarrior carrierborne bomber.

143

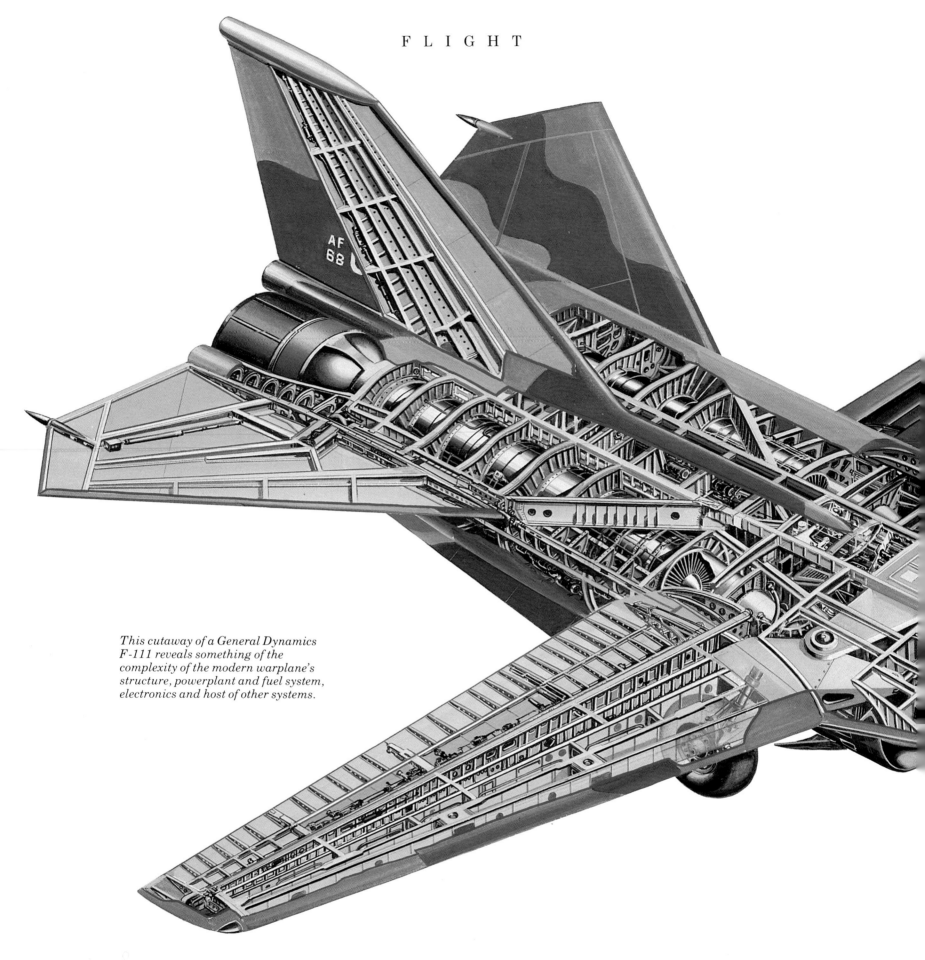

This cutaway of a General Dynamics F-111 reveals something of the complexity of the modern warplane's structure, powerplant and fuel system, electronics and host of other systems.

The US forces received at much the same time the firmly subsonic Vought A-7. This has the same basic configuration as the F8U (F-8) Crusader though without the variable-incidence wing, and as a result was designed and developed with great speed. The A-7 is operated by the US Air Force and US Navy (by which it is called the Corsair II) as a medium attack aircraft with great strength and payload plus a number of upgrade

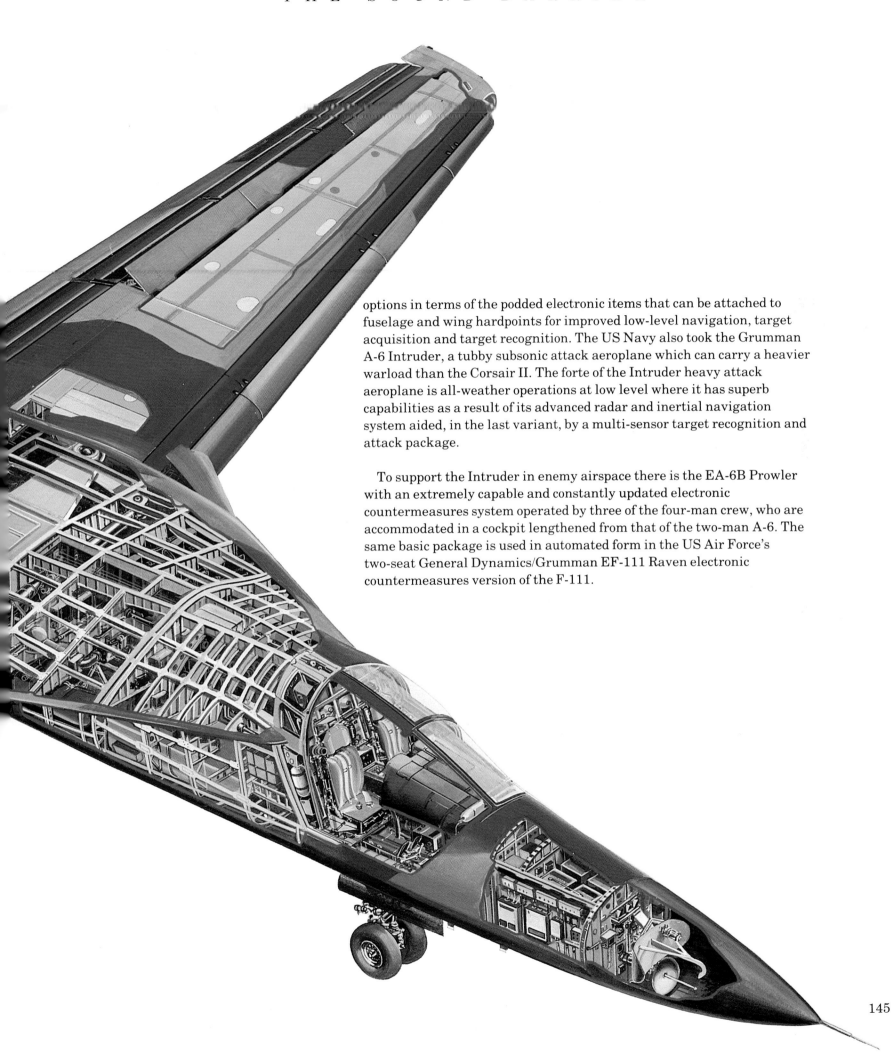

options in terms of the podded electronic items that can be attached to fuselage and wing hardpoints for improved low-level navigation, target acquisition and target recognition. The US Navy also took the Grumman A-6 Intruder, a tubby subsonic attack aeroplane which can carry a heavier warload than the Corsair II. The forte of the Intruder heavy attack aeroplane is all-weather operations at low level where it has superb capabilities as a result of its advanced radar and inertial navigation system aided, in the last variant, by a multi-sensor target recognition and attack package.

To support the Intruder in enemy airspace there is the EA-6B Prowler with an extremely capable and constantly updated electronic countermeasures system operated by three of the four-man crew, who are accommodated in a cockpit lengthened from that of the two-man A-6. The same basic package is used in automated form in the US Air Force's two-seat General Dynamics/Grumman EF-111 Raven electronic countermeasures version of the F-111.

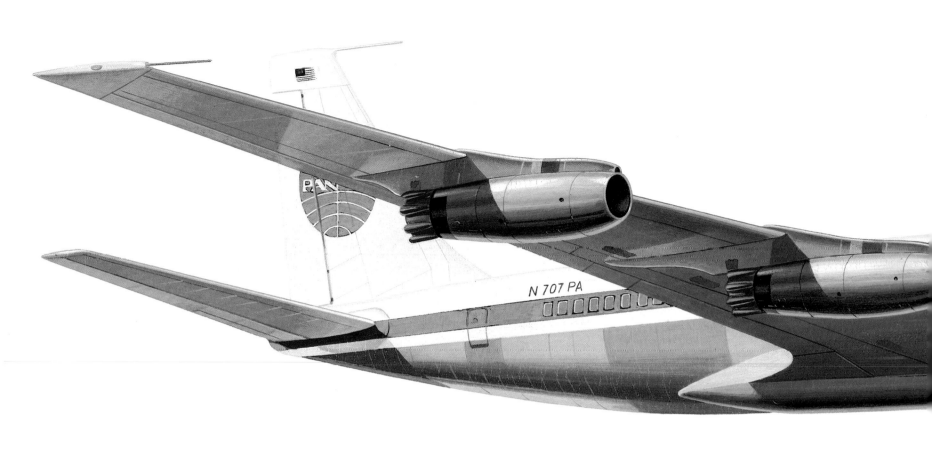

CHAPTER EIGHT:
CIVIL AVIATION

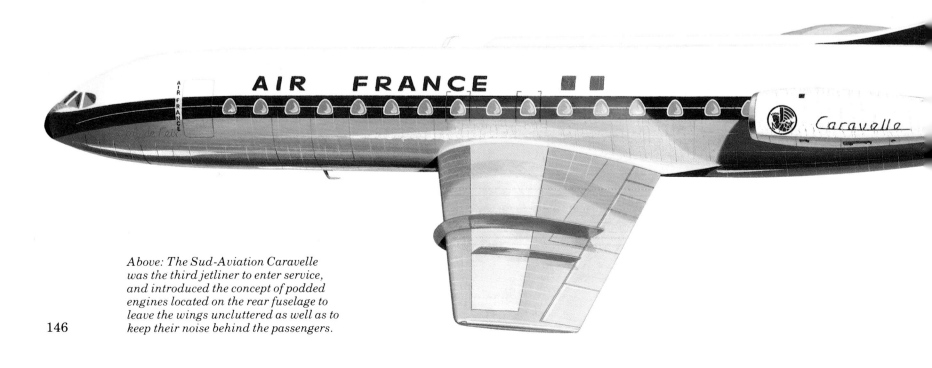

Above: The Sud-Aviation Caravelle was the third jetliner to enter service, and introduced the concept of podded engines located on the rear fuselage to leave the wings uncluttered as well as to keep their noise behind the passengers.

From the early 1960s civil air transport began to boom as the availability of long runways increased all over the world in line with deliveries of Boeing Model 707 and Douglas DC-8 long-range airliners. This boom was fuelled by the need of businessmen to travel as the economies of the major powers became more and more interdependent. Its wake prompted the growth of the travel industry, together with the creation of the package holiday business.

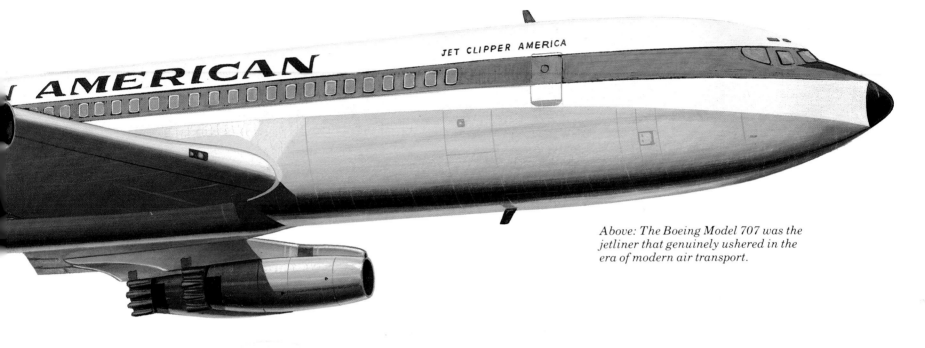

Above: The Boeing Model 707 was the jetliner that genuinely ushered in the era of modern air transport.

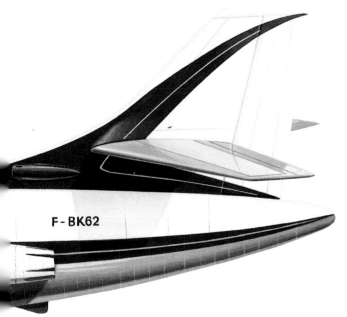

F-BK62

But hand-in-hand with this expansion of long-range travel came the growth of short- and medium-range air transport. These were required in their own right as part of the overall expansion of air transport and served as necessary adjuncts to long-range air transport, ensuring the regional movement of passengers into and out of any country's main airport or airports.

First in this field were the British with the ambitious BAC One-Eleven that stemmed from an original design by Hunting before that company was absorbed into BAC, now itself part of British Aerospace. At the core of the One-Eleven's design was the powerplant, which comprised a pair of Rolls-Royce Spey turbofans located on the sides of the rear fuselage. This type of engine is in essence a hybrid between the turbojet and the turboprop. A large-diameter forward fan driven by the turbine section provides, from its centre, the air needed by the engine and, from its outer section, what is in effect a tube of fast-flowing cold air, contained by the outer casing, which creates considerable thrust while smoothing out and cooling the hot exhaust gases. By comparison with the turbojet, therefore, the turbofan has a markedly greater diameter but produces more thrust, is quieter and gives far superior fuel economy. The rear position of these engines in the One-Eleven kept their noise to the rear of the passenger cabin and left the wing free for its prime purpose of generating lift in both its flight configuration and its take-off/landing configuration with high-lift devices deployed.

147

Above: The de Havilland Trident was a capable airliner that failed to win significant orders because it was too closely pitched at the requirement of British European Airways, its launch customer, to appeal to airlines with even slightly differing needs.

Left: The Dassaut Mercure was another airliner that failed to find a niche in an airliner market increasingly dominated by the offerings of Boeing and McDonnell Douglas.

Left: The Yakovlev Yak-42 is a simple Soviet airliner well matched to the USSR's need for civil aircraft able to operate from semi-prepared and even unprepared airstrips.

The One-Eleven suffered from a number of development problems, including difficulty of recovery from a deep stall because the tailplane of the T-tail design was blanketed, but then went on to secure a useful production run in a number of variants. These models were typical of the way civil aircraft were developing in this period, and in fact continue to develop. The initial variant had a cabin sized at the predicted capacity required by launch airlines, but was soon found to be too small to cater for the growing air travel market. So the fuselage was increased in length to allow the accommodation of more passengers. At the same time successively uprated engines were installed to allow operation at higher weights – carrying more passengers or more fuel – as well as from the airports increasingly to be found in hot and/or high regions where the thinner air adversely affects take-off performance.

But even as the Comet had been overhauled by the 707 and DC-8, the One-Eleven was passed by one Dutch and two American short-haul jetliners. The Dutch machine was the Fokker F.28 Fellowship using the same engine type and configuration as well as the same layout as the One-Eleven. The American machines were the Boeing 737 and the Douglas DC-9, the former with two turbofans in nacelles attached directly to the undersurface of the wing without any intervening pylons, and the latter with the now-familiar combination of a T-tail and engines located on the rear fuselage. All three of these short-haul types have proved immensely successful and have gone through numerous variants while remaining in production up to the present, though the Fellowship has become the fully modernized F100 with Rolls-Royce Tay turbofans in the same way that the twin-Dart F.27 has become the transformed F50 with twin Pratt & Whitney Canada PW125 turboprops.

149

While sales of the F.28 were steady if unspectacular – and look set to continue in much the same fashion with the F100 unless a partner is brought into the programme for co-production in the USA – those of the Model 737 and DC-9 have been spectacular. Both machines have been developed through variants with much increased passenger capacities and more powerful engines, Douglas leading the way with several options right from the beginning. The company had learned well the adverse lesson of offering the DC-8 with only a single length, and the availability of several fuselage options so boosted orders that the company found itself embarrassed by a lack of production capacity. This was one of the primary causes of the merger between Douglas and McDonnell in the late 1960s to create McDonnell Douglas, now one of the world's largest aerospace companies. It is impossible to overemphasize the importance of the 737 and DC-9 in the creation of today's air transport scene and development is continuing to maintain these two types in the forefront of their field for years to come. One of the options open to McDonnell Douglas is the replacement of the turbofan by the unducted fan, which is like a turbofan without its outer casing and with the forward fan replaced by a rear-mounted contra-rotating propeller unit for a reduction in fuel burn without sacrifice of performance.

Slightly further up the size and range scale comes the medium-haul type, and this airliner niche has been dominated by another Boeing aeroplane, the 727. This was designed from the outset to be independent of airport facilities and contains its own ventral airstair/door for loading and unloading of passengers as well as an auxiliary power unit for self-start capability. This allows it to make short hops with only a brief time on the ground. Capability is expanded by the plane's design with a T-tail, three turbofan engines (one in the base of the fin and the other two on the sides of the rear fuselage) and an advanced wing that allows high cruising speed

Above: The Boeing Model 737 is the world's best-selling airliner of all time, an unsophisticated short-range type that has proved itself to possess very considerable development potential.

Right: The Ilyushin Il-76 is one of the USSR's new generation of airlifters, a civil and military type designed for the carriage of freight over long ranges.

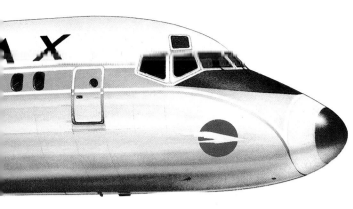

on medium-haul services as well as short-field performance of the type needed for many short-haul services. Until the development of the two latest 737 variants revitalized sales of this short-haul airliner, the 727 was the world's best-selling airliner and will remain one of the West's most important civil aircraft for many years to come.

The next step in the growth of civil aviation was the creation of the jumbo jet to cater for the enormous growth in long-range traffic during the 1960s. The machine that resulted is yet another Boeing design, the 747. The jumbo introduced the concept of the wide-body airliner, with a fuselage large enough in diameter to accommodate more than a single aisle and so providing, with its three longitudinal blocks of seats, a more spacious accommodation area. This effect has proved to be of considerable appeal to passengers and the basic physical parameters of the configuration are expanded by clever interior design and decor, with the galley and toilet facilities let into the partitions that separate the various

Top: The McDonnell Douglas equivalent to the Model 737, and also a best seller in its many forms, is the DC-9 with twin engines pod-mounted on the rear fuselage.

cabins to emphasize the cabin's division into what are in effect rooms. In the 747, this trend was enhanced by the provision of an extensively glazed first-class cabin in the extreme nose and the use of the substantial upper-deck fairing, aft of the flight deck, for additional first-class accommodation or a bar, reached from the lower deck by a spiral staircase. In this fashion Boeing managed to return in spirit and appeal to the Model 377 Stratocruiser that had proved so popular with passengers on long-distance flights.

The 747 was an enormous design challenge because of its size, but it is still an orthodox aeroplane that adheres to Boeing's well-proved formula for a long-distance airliner with moderately swept flying surfaces and four large engines located in pylon-mounted nacelles under and slightly forward of the wings. Such a location makes it easier to maintain the engines. It also makes it easy for the company to offer a choice of three engine marques to appeal to airlines with a strong affiliation to General Electric, Pratt & Whitney or Rolls-Royce. The 747 is still in large-scale production as Boeing produces yet more capable versions. Development is centred not so much on increasing capacity or performance, which are both on the plateaux demanded by the airlines, but on improving economy and reliability as a means of reducing operating costs. In the latest Model 747s Boeing has introduced the so-called two-man 'glass' cockpit with a few computer-controlled multi-function displays of the electronic flight instrumentation system to replace the mass of dials and switches of older models, an electronic flight-management system to control the flight by computer, drag-reducing winglets at the wingtips and other features designed to enhance an already high level of reliability.

Above: Designed and built by de Havilland's Australian subsidiary, the Drover found only a small market with operators such as the Royal Flying Doctor Service.

Top right: Designed and built by another de Havilland subsidiary, de Havilland Canada, the Beaver enjoyed considerable sales success as a rugged bushplane able to operate on wheel, ski or float alighting gear.

Below right: The Britten-Norman Islander is a no-frills light transport designed for complete reliability under primitive operating conditions.

152

HK-1009

AEROTAXI

VH-BPY

B

VH-BPY

BushPilots Airways

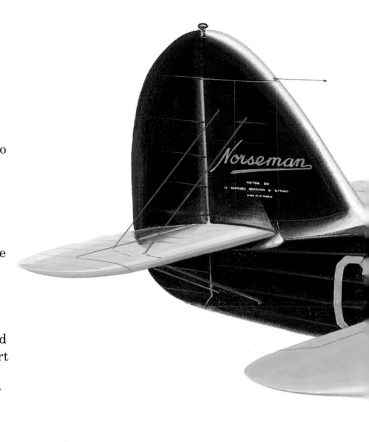

In the 1980s, the dominance of the American airliner has finally been challenged by the transport family produced by a European consortium, Airbus Industrie. The consortium is centred on British, French, Spanish and West German companies, and has made serious inroads into the previously American-dominated markets in Europe and the Far East, also doing well in Africa and South America. More recently it has begun to break into the market in North America. The Airbus family started with the A300, carrying up to 375 passengers over short and medium ranges, and developed through the A310, carrying up to 235 passengers over medium and long ranges, and the A320, carrying up to 180 passengers over short and medium ranges. These planes remain in production and are being developed into more advanced variants. The current family is to be augmented by the twin-engined A330 and four-engined A340 for long-range operations. The Airbus airliners have scored heavily with their reliability and operating economy, and have pioneered several operating systems (including a two-man cockpit with electronic instrumentation and fly-by-wire control system) as well as the use of composite materials in part replacement of aluminium and other metal alloys in the primary structure. Despite American assertions that they are priced competitively

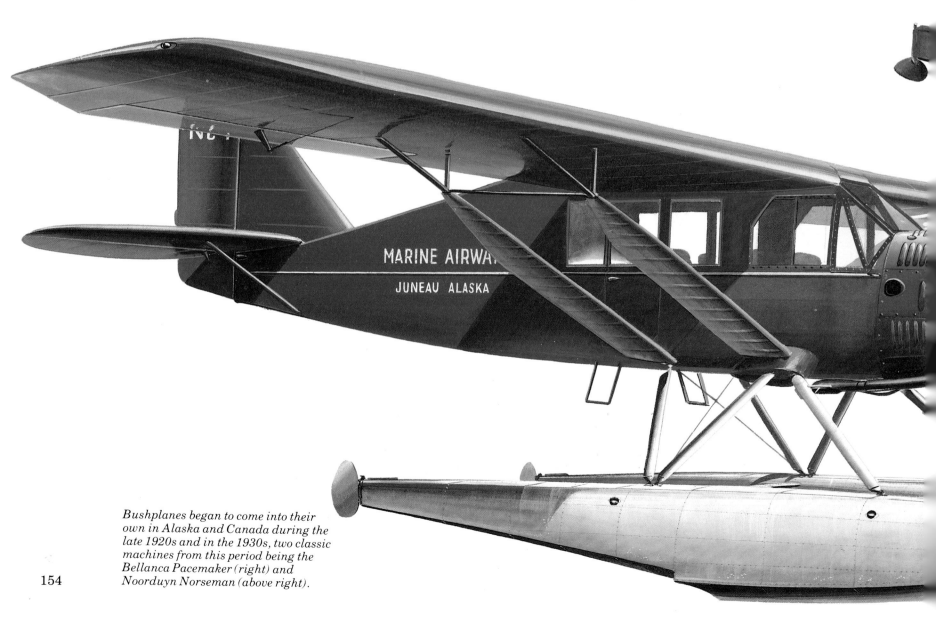

Bushplanes began to come into their own in Alaska and Canada during the late 1920s and in the 1930s, two classic machines from this period being the Bellanca Pacemaker (right) and Noorduyn Norseman (above right).

only because of government subsidies the Airbus airliners are now well established and taking significant market share from the American aerospace giants.

The Soviets have made determined efforts to secure an export market for their airliners in the various brackets filled by American and more recently by European aircraft, but have failed. The main problem appears to be the high structural weight and uneconomical engines of the Soviet airliners, which are expensive to operate. The problem has been compounded by the relatively poor reliability of Soviet engines, which require considerably more maintenance than their Western counterparts and keeps them out of service. Planes like the four-turboprop Ilyushin Il-18 and four-turbofan Il-62, the twin-turbofan Tupolev Tu-124, twin-turbofan Tu-134 and triple-turbofan Tu-154, and the triple-turbofan Yakovlev Yak-42 have been produced in large numbers only for the Eastern bloc countries and other allies.

It was clear as the 747 was being developed in the 1960s that there was also a market for a smaller-capacity airliner to operate over long ranges. Boeing lacked the capacity to enter into this market, which was ultimately satisfied by the Lockheed L-1011 TriStar and McDonnell Douglas DC-10. These two types have the same basic layout, with their three engines located as single units in two pylon-mounted underwing nacelles and the third engine at the tail, and both sold moderately well. However, the development of the TriStar nearly broke Lockheed and did, in fact, break its engine supplier, Rolls-Royce. Development difficulties and cost

overruns with the RB.211 were enormous and Rolls-Royce had finally to be rescued by the British government. It is worth noting, however, that the engine has gone on to become one of the major turbofans used by large airliners. Lockheed chose to drop out of the civil market, at least in the short term, after the troublesome TriStar programme, but the sudden upsurge in demand for air travel in the later 1980s has persuaded McDonnell Douglas to produce an updated version of the DC-10 – the MD-11, the redesignation terminating the world-famous DC series. (The DC-9's final developments have also been redesignated as the MD-80 series.) The MD-11 will not fly until 1990, but has already secured large orders.

Above: The primary logistic transport operated by the US Air Force is the Lockheed C-141 StarLifter, seen here in the form of a C-141A before its rebuild with a lengthened fuselage under the designation C-141B.

The next two aircraft from Boeing are the 757 and 767, which have a large degree of commonality but are respectively a narrow-body successor to the 727 with greater range and a wide-body equivalent carrying slightly fewer passengers over considerably greater range. Both types are full of advanced features, but though they are still at a relatively early stage of

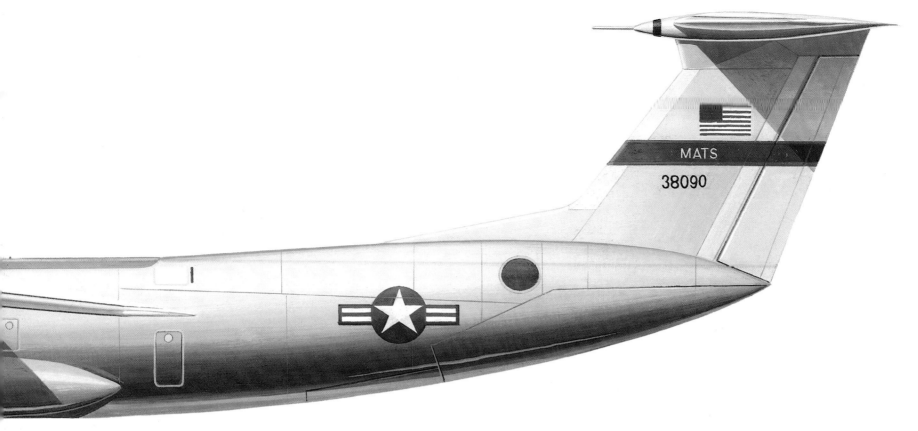

their development lives and operational careers, they are selling well and proving popular with passengers and airlines alike. Continued development will shortly produce models with different capacity and range options combined with reduced operating costs. This should ensure the continued importance of the two types in the airliner market.

Below: The US Air Force's most important long-range heavy transport is the Lockheed C-5 Galaxy, seen here in the form of the original C-5A type with a rear ramp and an upward-hingeing nose to permit straight-through loading and unloading of bulky items.

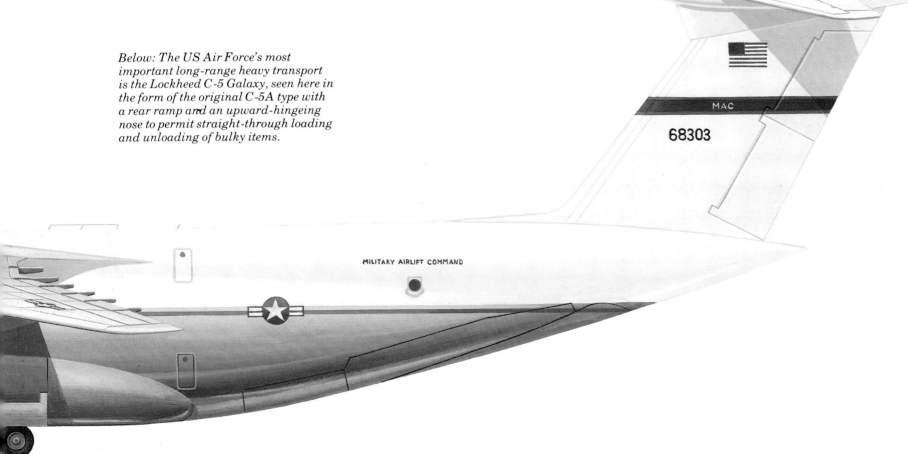

More recently, Soviet airliners have included the USSR's first wide-body plane, the four-turbofan Ilyushin Il-86. But even this has failed to break into the export market. However, greater success may attend the USSR's two latest airliners, the Il-96 development of the Il-86 and the twin-turbofan Tu-204. These more closely approximate Western airliners in direct operating costs, and the USSR may offer them at artificially low prices to attract customers.

Outside the mainstream of airliner development is the supersonic transport. This was never conceived as a vehicle for mass transport, but rather for the prestige low-volume/long-distance routes flown by businessmen and the like. America planned such a transport at the national level during the 1960s but did not proceed to the hardware stage. The Soviets produced the Tupolev Tu-144, but after a short time in service this was withdrawn for technical reasons – its exceptionally high

Above: The British Aircraft Corporation One-Eleven was one of the UK's most successful airliners, and production was later taken over by a Romanian industrial concern.

Below: The McDonnell Douglas DC-9 has found extensive favour with operators requiring a short/medium-range transport for the package-tour market.

operating costs was probably a further inducement for early retirement. This left the Anglo-French Concorde the world's sole supersonic transport. Developed and built jointly by Sud-Aviation and the British Aircraft Corporation, which are now parts of Aérospatiale and British Aerospace respectively, Concorde remains a great technical achievement. However, the manufacturers were deprived of large production orders by political antipathy and ecological opposition. The few aircraft built to production standard are flown by Air France and British Airways on their scheduled transatlantic services, operating profitably in this regime. They are also in constant demand for charter flights and other special purposes. However, there are moves for America to re-enter the supersonic transport market.

Right: The Boeing Model 727 was the world's most successful airliner until overtaken by the Model 737, and in addition to the standard side doors has a ventral airstair door for speed of loading and unloading.

Left: The Ilyushin Il-62 provides the USSR and Eastern European countries with their principal long-range passenger transport capability.

Below: The Yakolev Yak-42 is a simple yet effective short-range transport intended for use in areas offering few maintenance facilities.

Above: The British Aerospace 146 is a small/medium capacity airliner powered by four quiet turbofans for operation into and out of urban airports.

159

AIR CANADA

Below: McDonnell Douglas's competitor to the TriStar was the DC-10, another triple-engine type but in this instance with a choice of engine types. In the early 1990s airlines will begin to receive the completely updated MD-11 version of this airliner.

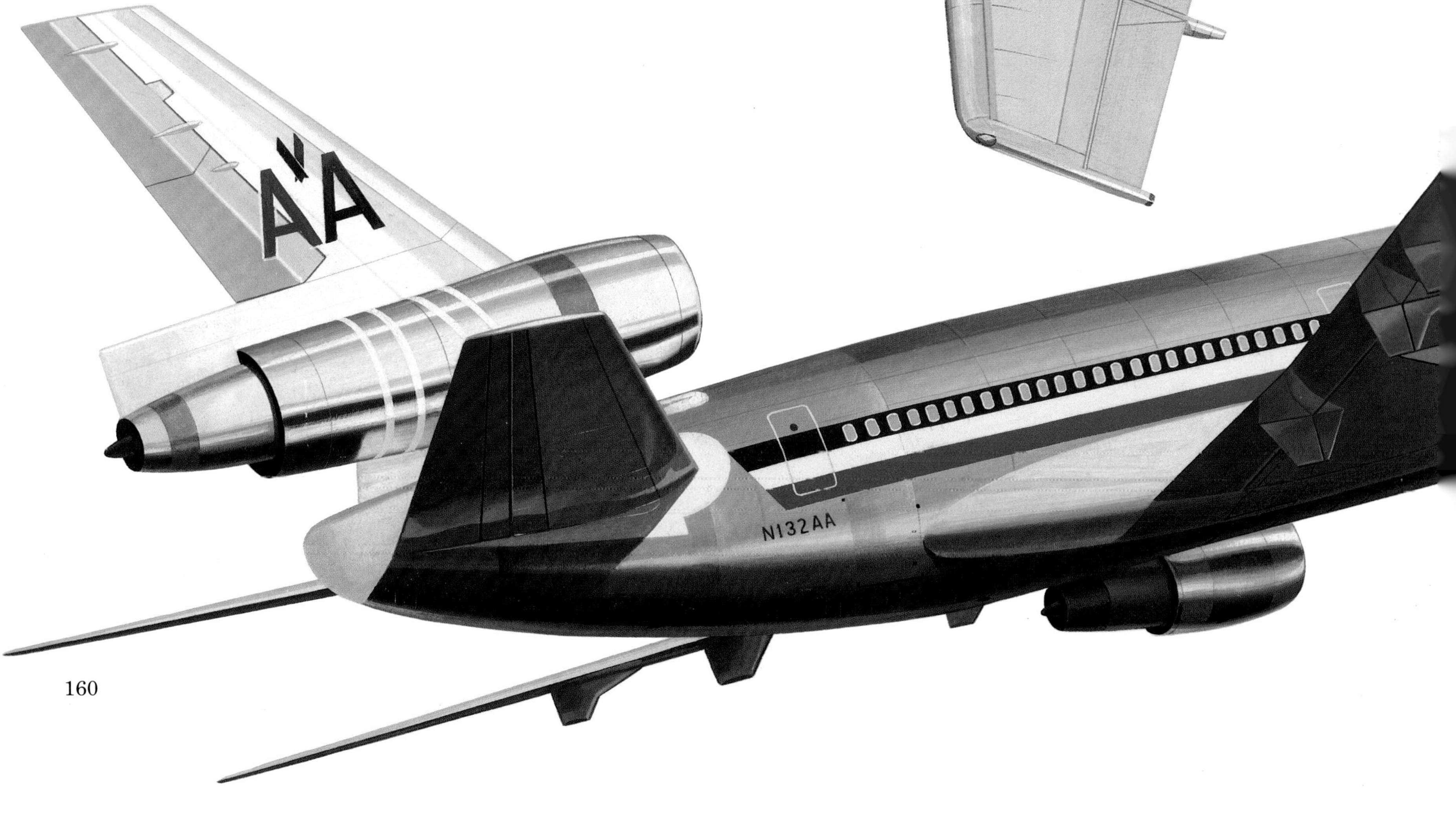

AA

N132AA

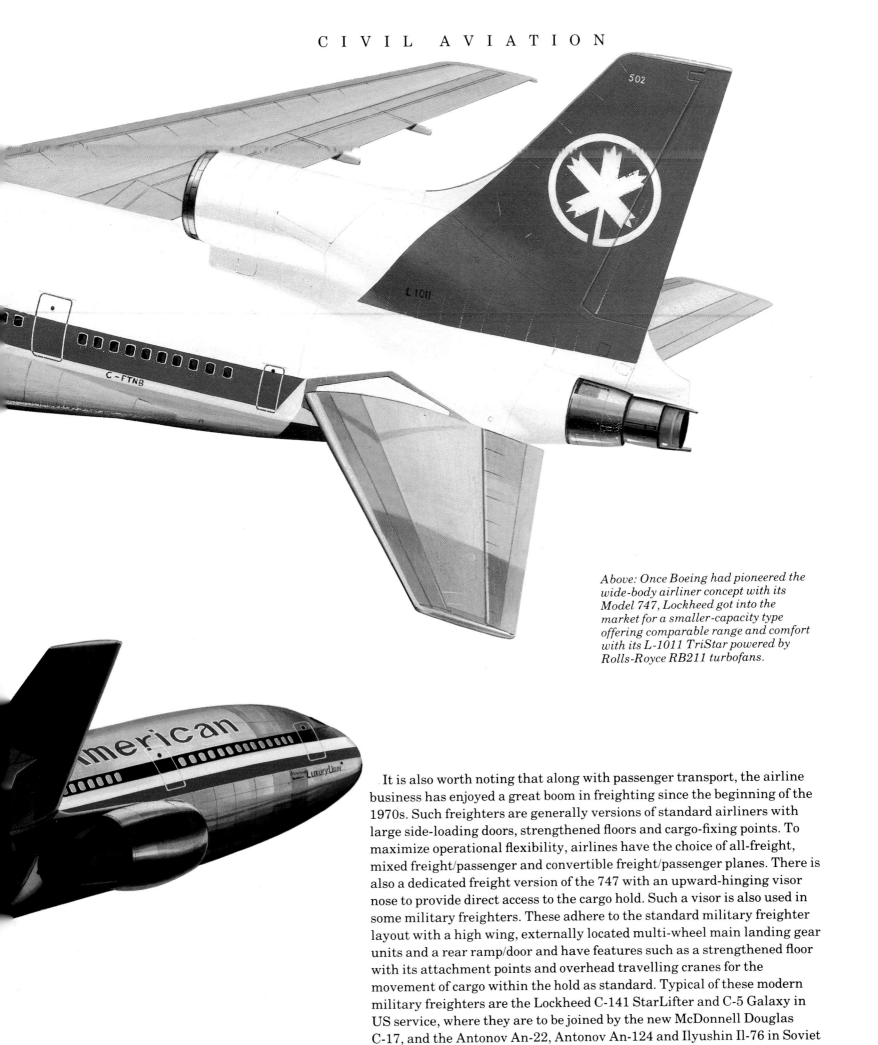

Above: Once Boeing had pioneered the wide-body airliner concept with its Model 747, Lockheed got into the market for a smaller-capacity type offering comparable range and comfort with its L-1011 TriStar powered by Rolls-Royce RB211 turbofans.

It is also worth noting that along with passenger transport, the airline business has enjoyed a great boom in freighting since the beginning of the 1970s. Such freighters are generally versions of standard airliners with large side-loading doors, strengthened floors and cargo-fixing points. To maximize operational flexibility, airlines have the choice of all-freight, mixed freight/passenger and convertible freight/passenger planes. There is also a dedicated freight version of the 747 with an upward-hinging visor nose to provide direct access to the cargo hold. Such a visor is also used in some military freighters. These adhere to the standard military freighter layout with a high wing, externally located multi-wheel main landing gear units and a rear ramp/door and have features such as a strengthened floor with its attachment points and overhead travelling cranes for the movement of cargo within the hold as standard. Typical of these modern military freighters are the Lockheed C-141 StarLifter and C-5 Galaxy in US service, where they are to be joined by the new McDonnell Douglas C-17, and the Antonov An-22, Antonov An-124 and Ilyushin Il-76 in Soviet service.

161

There are also, of course, a number of other civil air transports catering for the whole diversity of roles that has emerged in recent years, including the commuter, STOL and regional roles undertaken by the host of planes and variations to compete in this lively and growing market. The twin-turboprops for the commuter role include the EMBRAER EMB-110 from Brazil, the de Havilland Canada DHC-6 Twin Otter from Canada, the

The only supersonic airliner in service is the Anglo-French Concorde, a type produced jointly by British Aerospace and Aérospatiale (airframe) with Rolls-Royce and SNECMA (engines) for Air France and British Airways.

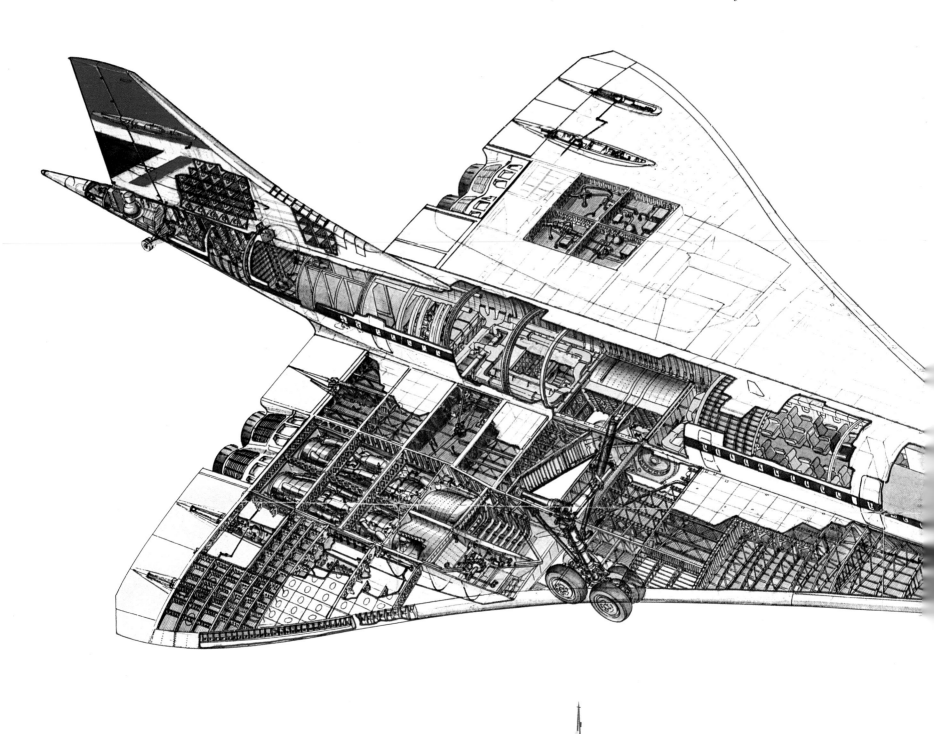

Shorts 330 and 360 from the UK, the Beech 1900 and Fairchild Metro from the USA, and the Dornier Do 228 from West Germany. The STOL market for airliners able to operate into city centres and airports surrounded by mountains is dominated by de Havilland Canada aircraft, most notably the DHC-7 Dash 7 and the DHC-8 Dash 8. Regional air transport is immensely competitive. Here major contenders include the EMBRAER EMB-120 from Brazil, the ATR-42 and ATR-72 from France and Italy, the CASA/IPTN CN-235 from Spain and Indonesia, the Saab 340 from Sweden, the BAe ATP from the UK, and the Antonov An-24 from the USSR. At the upper end of the market, there is even the BAe 146 which operates in the short-range market as a four-turbofan type of exceptional quietness.

Civil aviation today also encompasses various types of business aeroplane (powered by piston, turboprop, turbojet and turbofan engines), light aircraft of many types, agricultural aircraft, sporting/aerobatic aircraft and gliders, and a host of helicopters used in a variety of tasks ranging from support of the offshore industry to air ambulance work.

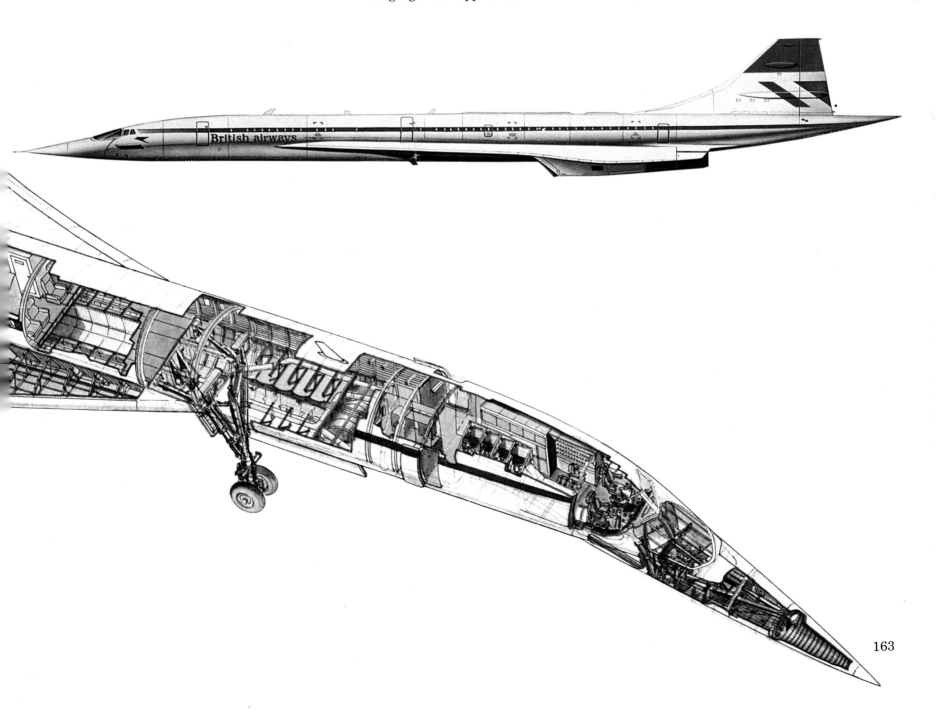

163

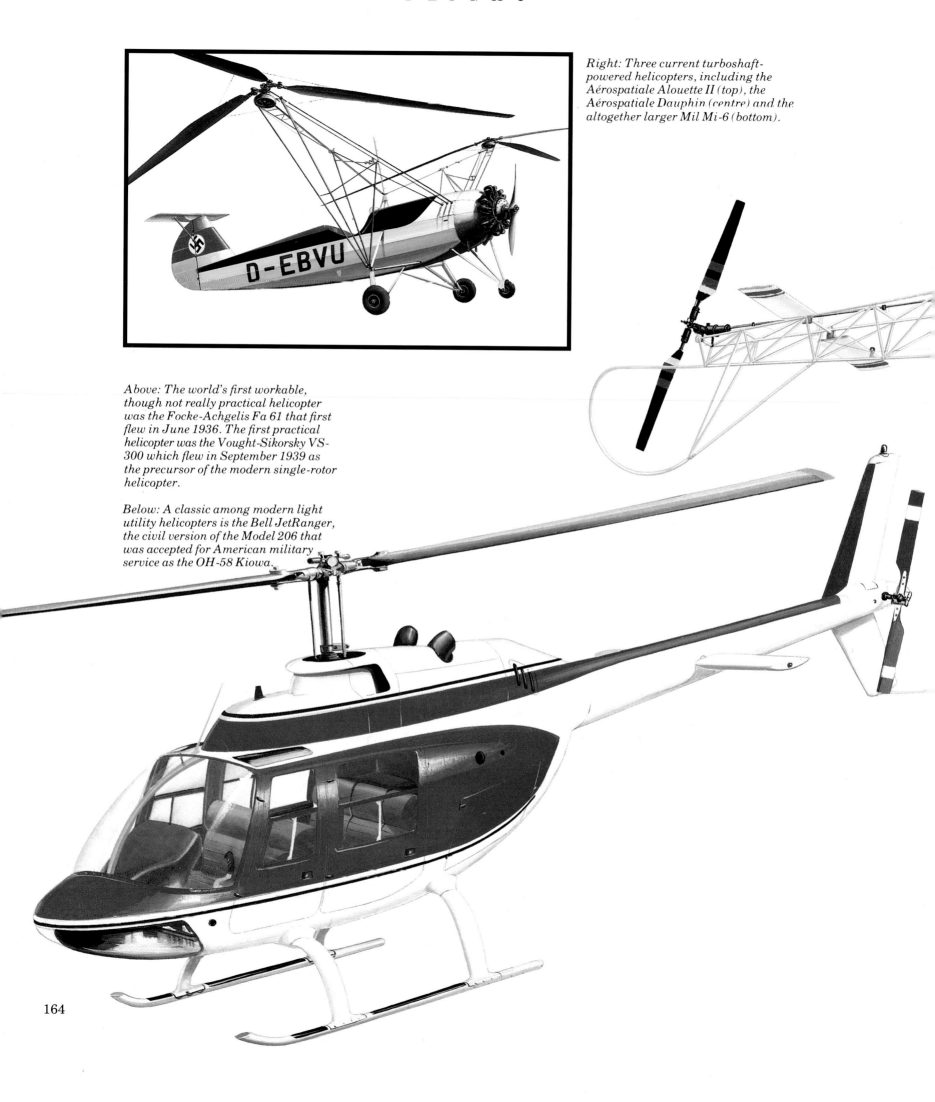

Right: Three current turboshaft-powered helicopters, including the Aérospatiale Alouette II (top), the Aérospatiale Dauphin (centre) and the altogether larger Mil Mi-6 (bottom).

Above: The world's first workable, though not really practical helicopter was the Focke-Achgelis Fa 61 that first flew in June 1936. The first practical helicopter was the Vought-Sikorsky VS-300 which flew in September 1939 as the precursor of the modern single-rotor helicopter.

Below: A classic among modern light utility helicopters is the Bell JetRanger, the civil version of the Model 206 that was accepted for American military service as the OH-58 Kiowa.

Below: The Boeing Vertol CH-47 Chinook has two rotors (one at each end of the fuselage driven by twin turboshafts located on the sides of the rear rotor pylon) for a large payload carried internally or externally.

Left: The McDonnell Douglas Helicopters (previously Hughes) AH-64 Apache is currently the western world's most advanced battlefield helicopter, a sophisticated type possessing great power and advanced sensors for the delivery of weapons such as the Hellfire anti-tank missile.

Above: The Sikorsky HH-53 Super Jolly is the combat search and rescue version of the CH-53 Stallion assault transport helicopter. Among its features are a retractable inflight-refuelling probe, advanced electronics, weapons, armour protection and a rescue hoist.

167

Right: Advances in turbofan technology have made large twin-engined airliners a safe and economic reality, and among the manufacturers who have stepped into this market is Boeing with its Model 767.

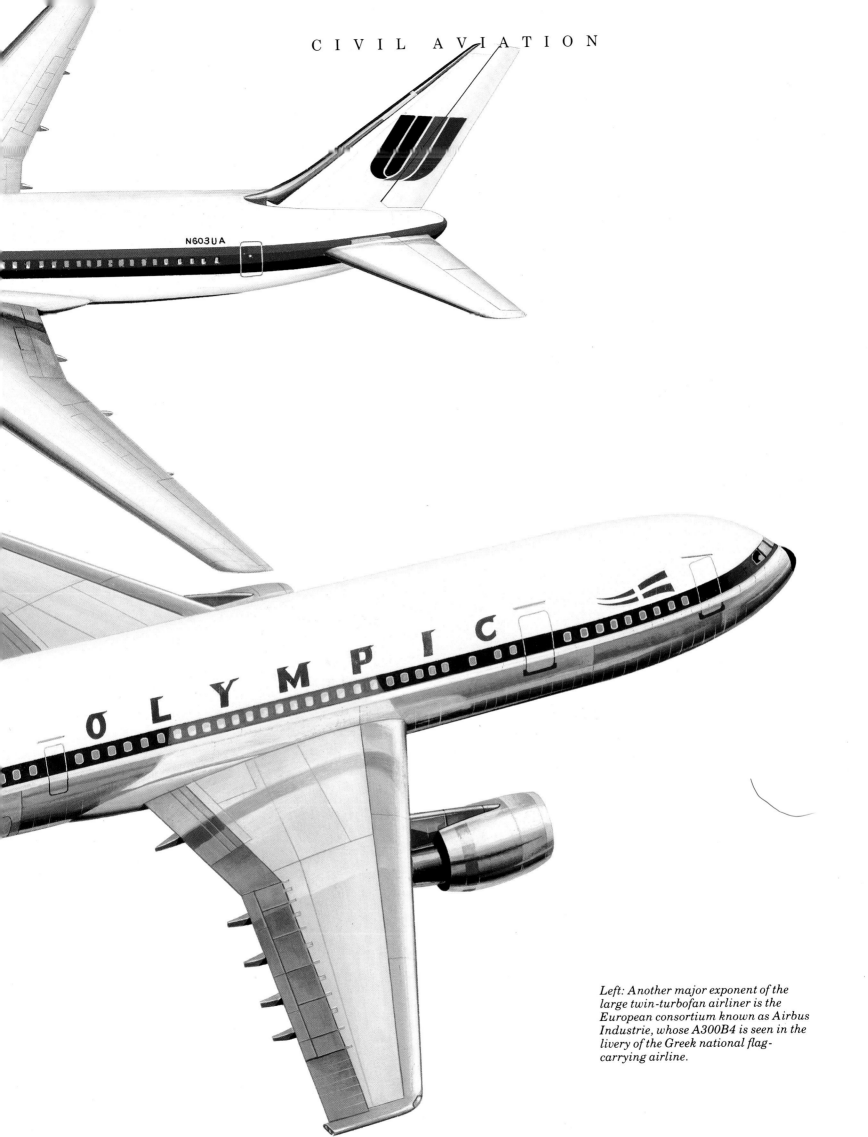

N603UA

OLYMPIC

Left: Another major exponent of the large twin-turbofan airliner is the European consortium known as Airbus Industrie, whose A300B4 is seen in the livery of the Greek national flag-carrying airline.

169

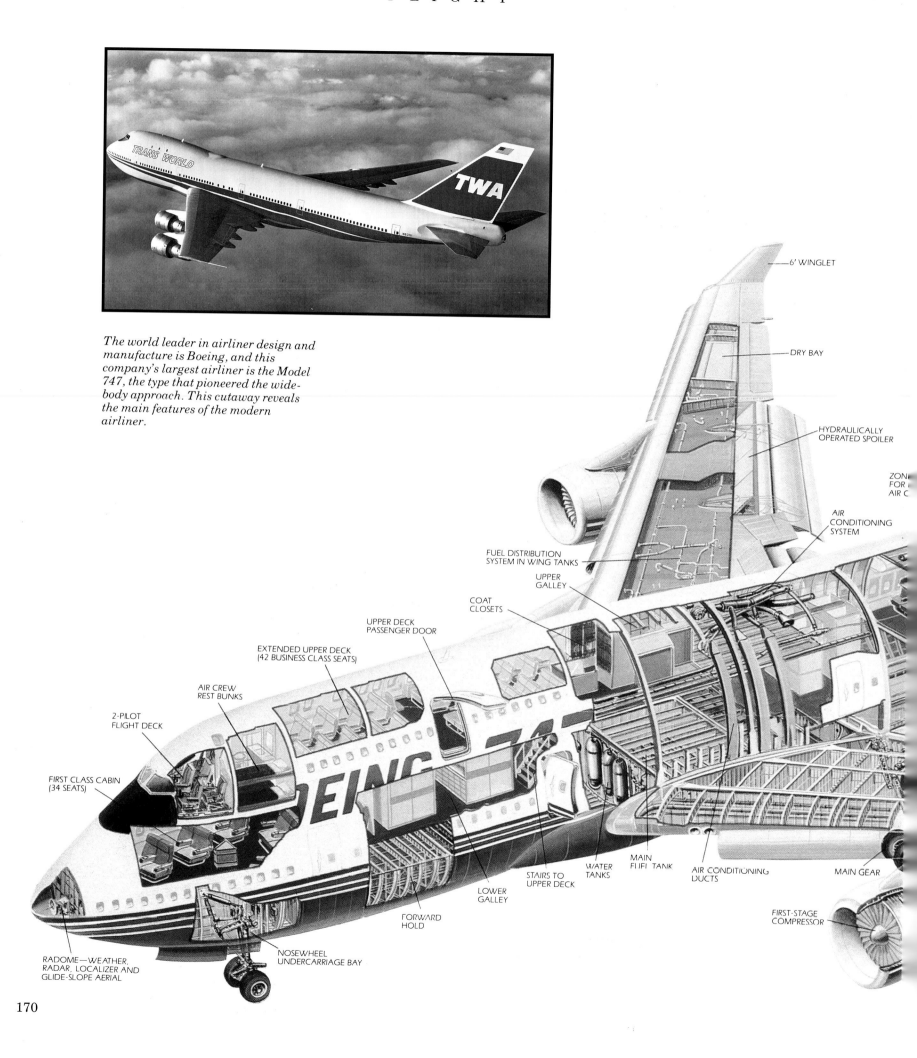

The world leader in airliner design and manufacture is Boeing, and this company's largest airliner is the Model 747, the type that pioneered the wide-body approach. This cutaway reveals the main features of the modern airliner.

6' WINGLET

DRY BAY

HYDRAULICALLY OPERATED SPOILER

ZON
FOR
AIR C

AIR CONDITIONING SYSTEM

FUEL DISTRIBUTION SYSTEM IN WING TANKS

UPPER GALLEY

COAT CLOSETS

UPPER DECK PASSENGER DOOR

EXTENDED UPPER DECK (42 BUSINESS CLASS SEATS)

AIR CREW REST BUNKS

2-PILOT FLIGHT DECK

FIRST CLASS CABIN (34 SEATS)

STAIRS TO UPPER DECK

WATER TANKS

MAIN FUEL TANK

AIR CONDITIONING DUCTS

MAIN GEAR

LOWER GALLEY

FORWARD HOLD

FIRST-STAGE COMPRESSOR

RADOME—WEATHER, RADAR, LOCALIZER AND GLIDE-SLOPE AERIAL

NOSEWHEEL UNDERCARRIAGE BAY

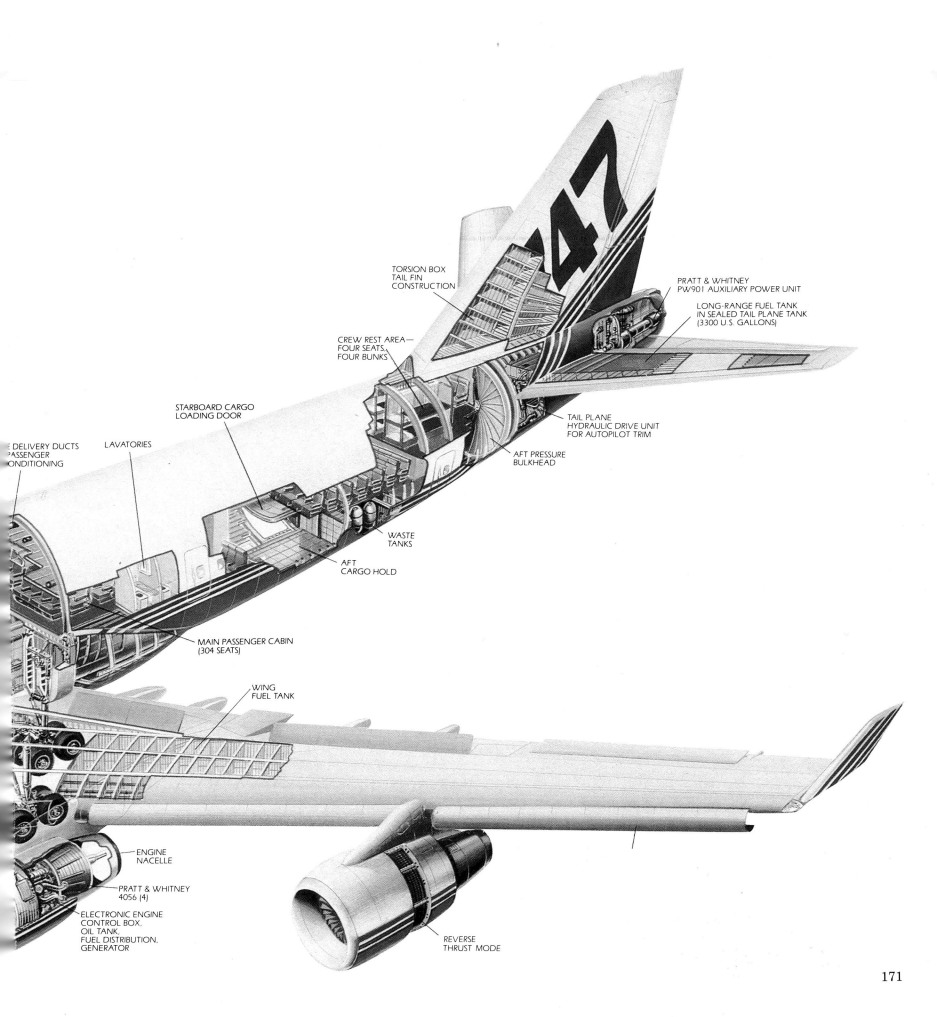

TORSION BOX
TAIL FIN
CONSTRUCTION

PRATT & WHITNEY
PW901 AUXILIARY POWER UNIT

LONG-RANGE FUEL TANK
IN SEALED TAIL PLANE TANK
(3300 U.S. GALLONS)

CREW REST AREA—
FOUR SEATS,
FOUR BUNKS

STARBOARD CARGO
LOADING DOOR

TAIL PLANE
HYDRAULIC DRIVE UNIT
FOR AUTOPILOT TRIM

E DELIVERY DUCTS
PASSENGER
ONDITIONING

LAVATORIES

AFT PRESSURE
BULKHEAD

WASTE
TANKS

AFT
CARGO HOLD

MAIN PASSENGER CABIN
(304 SEATS)

WING
FUEL TANK

ENGINE
NACELLE

PRATT & WHITNEY
4056 (4)

ELECTRONIC ENGINE
CONTROL BOX,
OIL TANK,
FUEL DISTRIBUTION,
GENERATOR

REVERSE
THRUST MODE

CHAPTER NINE: THE PRESENT

There is enormous growth in aviation at the present both in the military and civilian fields. But it is hampered strongly by the enormous costs of designing, developing and producing any new combat aeroplane. One of the results of this increase in the financial burden has been the growth of collaborative projects between companies – as in the USA for the new tactical fighters being planned for the US Air Force and US Navy – or between nations, as is the case with a number of European aircraft. There is also an increasing tendency to pull in a nation from the developing world. This helps the major partner to secure an export market and the minor partner to expand his own technological base.

At the operational level the watershed for modern military aircraft was the Vietnam War, which clearly revealed the failings of the US-inspired concept of outright performance above all other factors. Vietnam showed that tactical aircraft still require agility and ease of maintenance. It also showed that, in any real war, an advanced air force must possess a

One of the most impressive of modern warplanes is the McDonnell Douglas F-15 Eagle, designed as a fast-climbing air superiority fighter but now in service as a multi-role type.

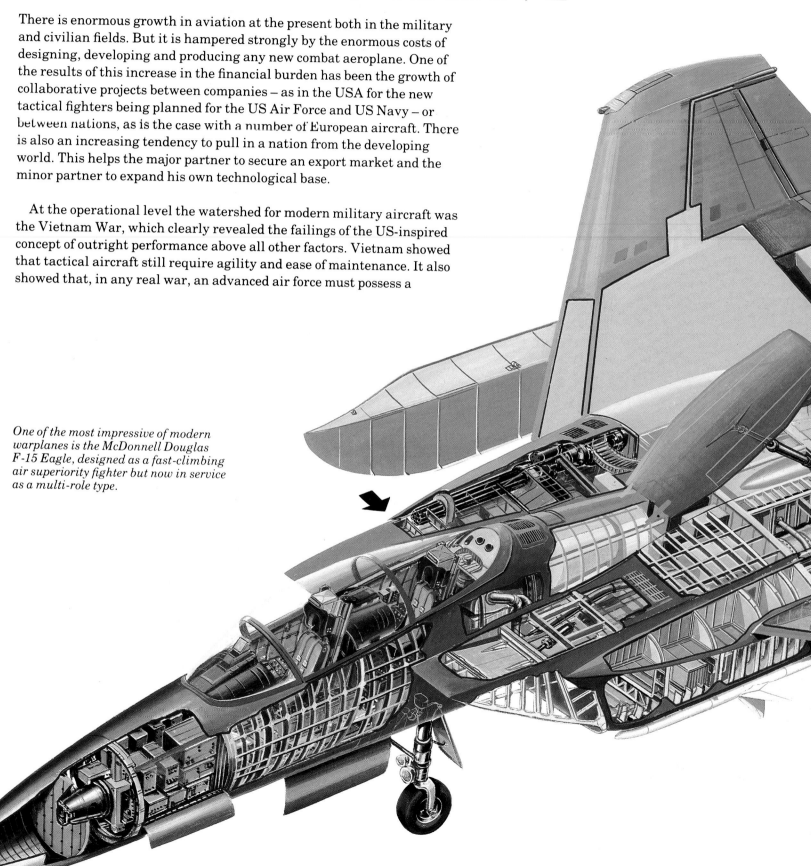

judicious blend of aircraft that include interceptors and air-superiority fighters, characterized by outright performance, and tactical fighters in which sheer speed and altitude requirements are far less important than factors such as instantaneous and sustained turn rates, rate of climb and low-level acceleration.

The nation that led the way was of course the USA. For the air force and navy interception/air-superiority role there emerged the McDonnell Douglas F-15 Eagle and Grumman F-14 Tomcat respectively. Both of them are large twin-turbofan planes with advanced radar and weapons. The Tomcat also has variable-geometry wings for low carrier approach speed but high dash speed. Their agile air-combat and tactical fighters include the air force's General Dynamics F-16 Fighting Falcon and the navy's McDonnell Douglas F/A-18 Hornet. These have electronically controlled 'fly-by-wire' flight control systems, in which a computer translates the pilot's control column movements into the most appropriate movements of the control surfaces. This allows the basic stability of the aircraft to be relaxed to the point of instability, resulting in phenomenal agility combined with high – but not Mach 2+ – performance as well as allowing an exceptionally diverse assortment of externally carried weapons.

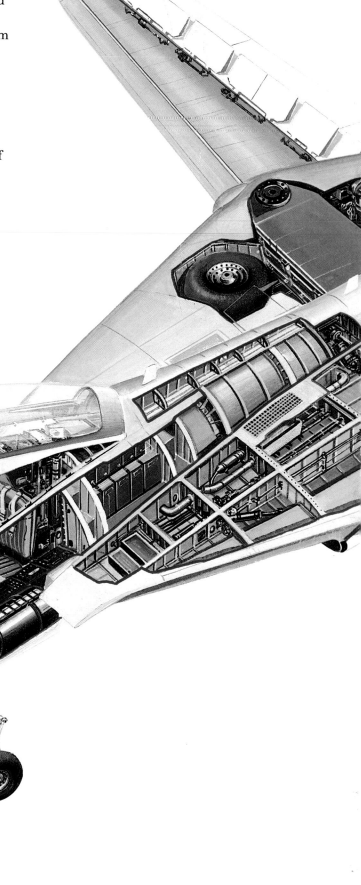

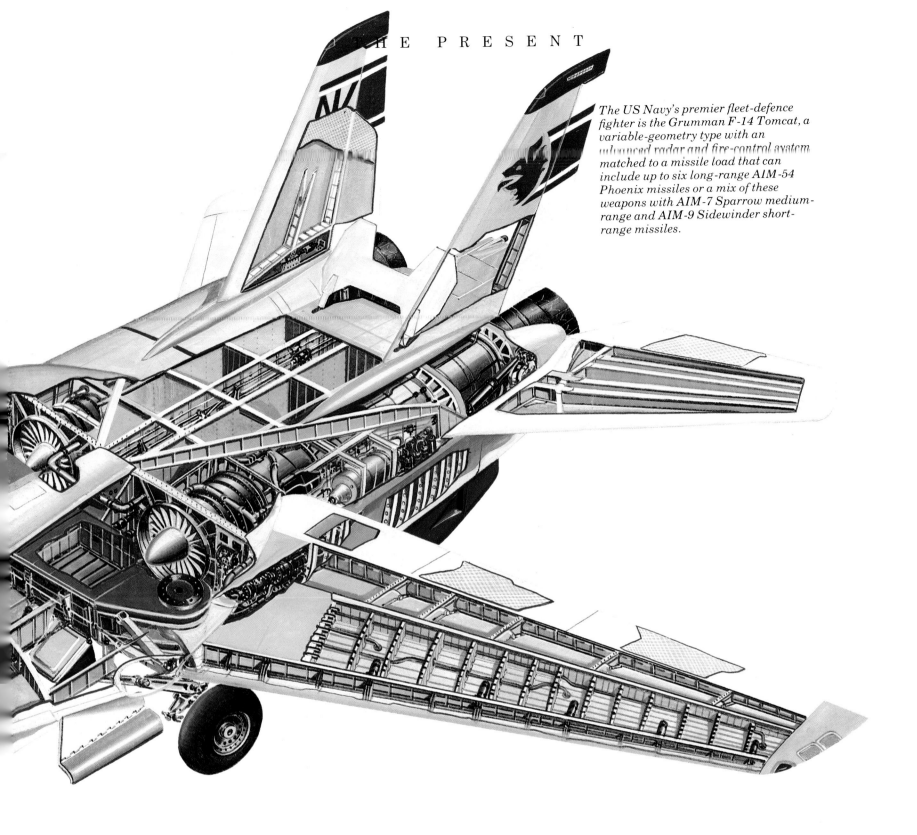

The US Navy's premier fleet-defence fighter is the Grumman F-14 Tomcat, a variable-geometry type with an advanced radar and fire-control system matched to a missile load that can include up to six long-range AIM-54 Phoenix missiles or a mix of these weapons with AIM-7 Sparrow medium-range and AIM-9 Sidewinder short-range missiles.

The F-15 has also been developed into the potent F-15E long-range interdiction plane with a two-man crew and additional weapon-carriage capability on hardpoints mounted tangentially on the big but low-drag exterior fuel tanks attached to the flanks of the engine inlet trunks. Experiments are also being made with thrust-vectoring nozzles on the engines to produce very short take-off/landing runs and increased agility in combat. It is also likely that the F-16 will form the basis for a new battlefield close-support aircraft to replace the Fairchild Republic A-10 Thunderbolt II. This is an aeroplane of devastating offensive power with its air-to-surface missiles and seven-barrel 30-mm cannon firing depleted uranium anti-tank projectiles, but is firmly subsonic.

After its fighters were revealed in the Vietnam War as too complex, heavy and sophisticated, the US Air Force launched a programme to produce a lighter yet more versatile fighter. The result is the General Dynamics F-16 Fighting Falcon, a design with blended aerodynamics and relaxed stability controlled by the pilot in his semi-reclining seat by means of a fly-by-wire system.

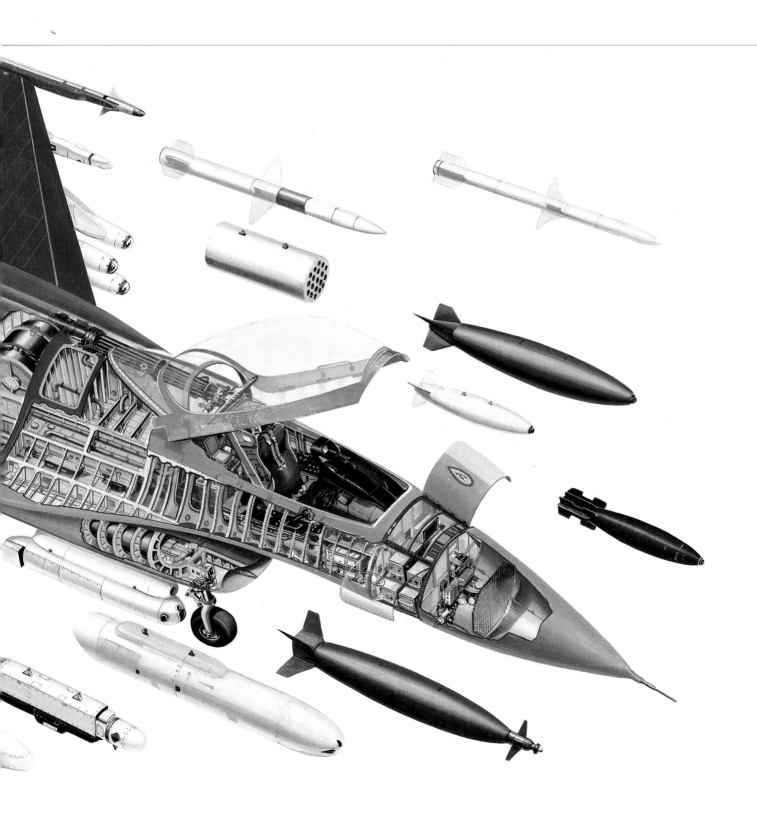

The USSR has moved along similar lines, steadily closing the technological gap between its aircraft and those of the USA. The Mikoyan-Gurevich MiG-21 fighter was succeeded by the variable-geometry MiG-23. The Sukhoi Su-15 interceptor was supplemented by the MiG-25 – a Mach 3 high-altitude plane designed to counter the North American B-70, and eventually modernized as the MiG-31 for low-altitude interception of cruise missiles. The MiG-27 was developed from the MiG-23 as a ground-attack fighter. The Su-7 was developed with variable-geometry wings as the Su-17, Su-20 and Su-22. The Su-25 was produced as the Soviet equivalent to the Thunderbolt II. And the variable-geometry Su-24 was developed as a long-range interdictor equivalent to the F-111. Further developments in the last few years have added the MiG-29 and Su-27 as advanced air-combat and air-superiority fighters in much the same basic roles as the Fighting Falcon and Eagle.

European efforts have also produced some interesting planes, the oldest among them being the BAe Harrier, the world's first operational aeroplane

Above: The Fairchild Republic A-10 Thunderbolt II is a dedicated tank-killing aeroplane with only modest performance but considerable agility and protection to optimize the aeroplane's chances of engaging battlefield targets with its massive 30-mm seven-barrel cannon and large load of ordnance carried on 11 external hardpoints.

Below: The Grumman EA-6B Prowler is the electronic warfare counterpart of the A-6 Intruder carrierborne attack bomber, and designed to shield US Navy attack forces with its internal ALQ-99 electronic warfare system and external jammer pods.

with the ability to take-off and land vertically by vectoring the thrust from the four engine nozzles grouped around the centre of gravity. The forward pair are fed with cold air from the fan stage of the Rolls-Royce Pegasus turbofan, and the rear pair with hot gases from the turbine stage of the engine. With the nozzles directed straight down the Harrier is pushed upward into the air, where a rotation of the nozzles to the rear accelerates the aeroplane forward until it is supported by its wings. Reversing this process allows the plane to land vertically too. The operational advantages of such a VTOL type are enormous. The Harrier does not need a conventional runway and, with its support equipment, can be deployed away from vulnerable airfields. The basic Harrier has undergone considerable development in the 1970s and 1980s, but is now being superseded by an altogether more advanced derivative, developed jointly by BAe and McDonnell Douglas with a larger wing of composite construction, a more powerful engine, better lift-improvement devices, a new cockpit and a host of other upgraded features. This new model is used by the Royal Air Force as the Harrier GR.Mk 5, and by the US Marine Corps as the AV-8B Harrier II. It is worth noting that vertical take-off is seldom used as it restricts maximum take-off weight to the total thrust of the engines. More common is a short take-off, where the heavily laden aeroplane is accelerated for about 250 or 300 yards. Then the nozzles are turned sharply down to throw the aeroplane upward and into the air with a combination of aerodynamic lift and direct thrust.

This STOVL method of operation is also standard for the Sea Harrier naval version, which was designed for the fighter, reconnaissance and strike roles. It has a completely different fighter-type cockpit and instrumentation, radar, other specialist electronics and a revised suite of weapons. This has proved its capabilities in combat against aircraft with higher performance, and is operated from the UK's small aircraft-carriers which have a raised 'ski jump' forward section to their flight decks to throw the accelerating Sea Harrier upward into the air. Further development of such STOVL aircraft is inevitable and, indeed, overdue. The Soviets already field the Yakovlev Yak-38 as an interim naval plane, and the British/American partners are considering a supersonic STOVL warplane.

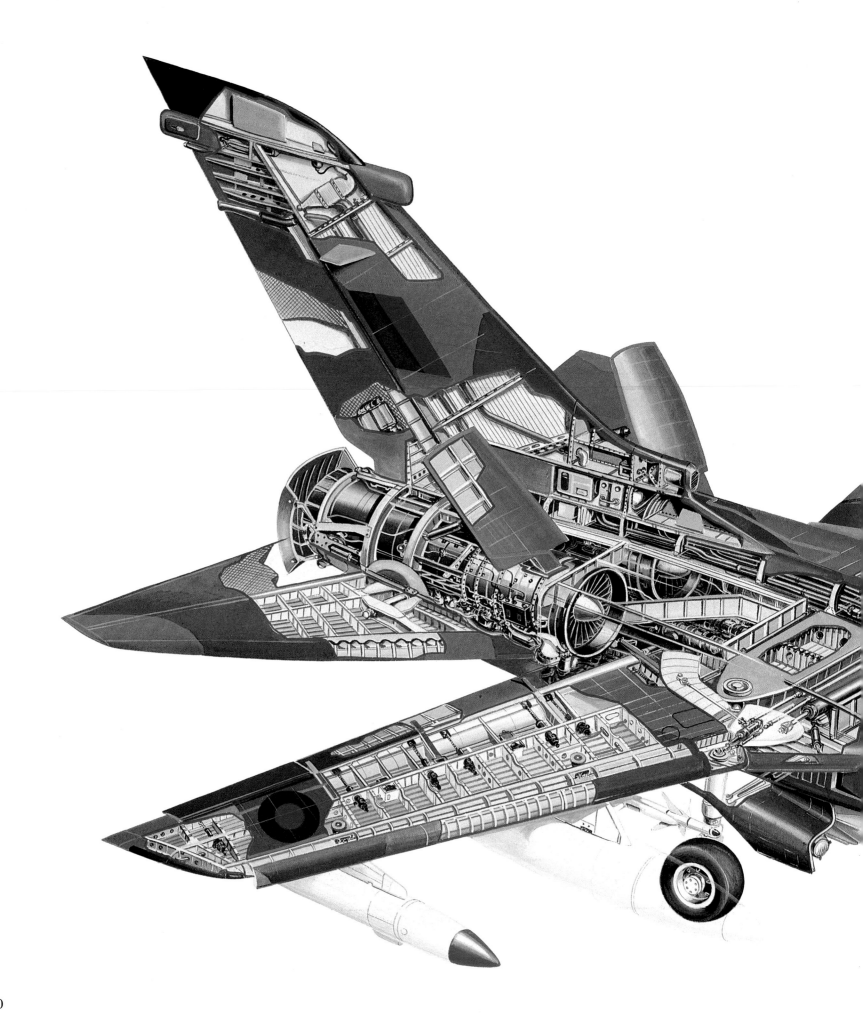

The Panavia Tornado, designed and
produced by a consortium of British,
Italian and West German interests, is a
high-performance interdictor intended
to penetrate heavily defended airspace
at high speed and very low level for the
delivery of heavy ordnance loads with
pinpoint accuracy.

Other European warplanes are in service or in the pipeline. Most
capable of the current generation is the Panavia Tornado, a joint
development by the British, Italian and West German aerospace
industries as a multi-role type with variable-geometry wings and STOL
performance. The Tornado was first fielded in the interdiction role, where
the keys to its success are the ability to fly long distances at supersonic
speed at very low altitude with a heavy warload. The Tornado has a very
advanced navigation and attack system, allowing extreme precision of
attack on a single pass, and has also secured useful export orders. For use
with the Boeing E-3 Sentry AWACS (Airborne Warning And Control
System) aeroplane – a powerful 'force multiplier' that can see
electronically deep into enemy territory and control all air operations
within several hundreds of miles – the British have developed an
air-defence variant of the Tornado, while the Italians and West Germans

Produced jointly by McDonnell Douglas and British Aerospace, the AV-8B Harrier II is a radical development of the all-British Harrier STOVL warplane with a more advanced cockpit, a larger wing, enhanced lift-improvement devices and other features for greater combat radius with a considerably larger warload.

are producing an electronic combat and reconnaissance variant. Other possibilities include a maritime attack model, and the Tornado is still full of enough development potential to remain important until well into the next century.

Sweden has produced the Saab 37 Viggen as a highly sophisticated multi-role type. This canard aeroplane has genuine STOL capability so that it can be deployed to short stretches of road. It is to be supplemented and then supplanted in the 1990s by the more ambitious lightweight Saab 39 Gripen, another canard plane for STOL performance and aerial agility, in this instance promoted by a fly-by-wire control system.

France has produced several successful types in succession to the Mirage III and 5 family. First came the Dassault-Breguet Mirage F1, a dual-role

183

fighter and ground-attack type of more conventional layout than the delta-winged Mirage III and 5 to avoid the latter's drag-induced loss of performance at low altitude or in a turning flight. It has emulated the Mirage III/5's export success and is now being followed by the Dassault-Breguet Mirage 2000. This returns to the delta layout, but in this instance with a combination of relaxed stability and fly-by-wire controls to ensure no degradation of performance in low-altitude or turning combat. To succeed the Etendard IVM naval fighter, Dassault-Breguet produced the modernized Super Etendard with nose radar and the potent Exocet anti-ship missile. But this and several landplane fighters are to be replaced from the mid-1990s by variants of the Dassault-Breguet Rafale new-generation fighter, a canard type with fly-by-wire controls, a large measure of composite construction, advanced electronics and a high power-to-weight ratio for good straight-line and turning performance.

Italy, Spain, the UK and France are producing a comparable though slightly heavier type as the Eurofighter EFA. With Brazil, Italy has produced the AMX light attack fighter with less sophisticated electronics and smaller size to reduce both development and purchase costs. A comparable though less advanced machine is the result of a Romanian and Yugoslav collaboration, called the IAR-93 and Orao respectively in the two countries.

At the heavier end of the warplane range, the bombers, only the USA and USSR are active. The USA has long relied on the B-52, but this is now decidedly obsolescent and being supplanted by the Rockwell B-1B, a variable-geometry bomber designed to penetrate enemy airspace at ground-hugging altitude before firing its cruise missiles. The B-1B is to be relegated to the more conventional bombing role when the USA's latest bomber, the Northrop B-2, begins to enter service in the 1990s. This

Above right: Produced by Romania and Yugoslovia, and known in those countries as the IAR-93 and Orao respectively, this is an unsophisticated yet effective light attack aeroplane.

Below: The Dassault-Breguet Atlantic is a very long-ranged maritime patroller that has recently been updated and returned to production as the more formidable Atlantique 2.

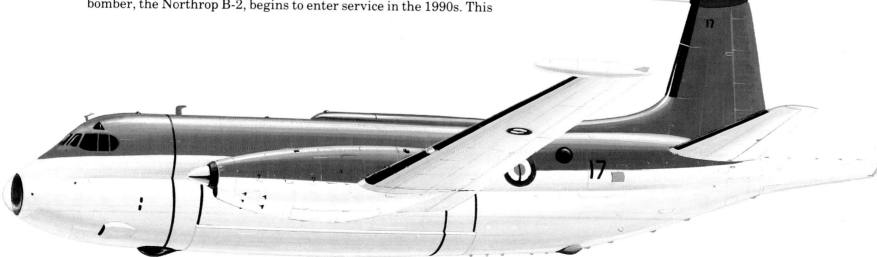

Below: Retaining an aerodynamic similarity to the Mirage III, the Dassault-Breguet Mirage 2000 is an altogether new combat aeroplane with a fly-by-wire control system, capable radar and modern weapons.

Bottom: The Saab 37 Viggen is matched precisely to Sweden's particular defence needs, and uses a combination of canard layout, strong landing gear and a thrust-reversible turbofan to provide the capability for dispersed operations from and into short lengths of road.

subsonic flying-wing plane is of the 'stealth' type, designed neither to radiate nor to reflect the electro-magnetic or thermal energies generally used to detect modern aircraft. The Americans have poured vast sums into the development of this monumentally advanced plane and have high hopes for it.

The Soviets' two most advanced bombers are the fixed-wing Tupolev Tu-26 and the variable-geometry Tu-160. Though both are strategic bombers. The former is a medium-range type intended mainly for the theatre or maritime role, while the latter is a long-range type armed with cruise missiles for the intercontinental task.

Then there are the anti-submarine aircraft, which fall into land- and carrier-based types. The major land-based aircraft are the British BAe

Recent developments in military technology have been concentrated on reducing the 'observability' of warplanes, and a striking example of the new concept is the Lockheed F-117, a radarless attacker intended to penetrate into enemy airspace without being detected to destroy a high-value target with its precision-guided weapons.

Nimrod, based on the aerodynamics of the Comet airliner and powered by four turbofans; the French Dassault-Breguet Atlantic 1 and its successor the Atlantique 2 with two turboprops; the Soviet Ilyushin Il-38 and Tupolev Tu-95 each with four turboprops; and the US Lockheed P-3 Orion with four turboprops. This last is to be radically updated and upgraded as the virtually new P-7 in the 1990s. As far as carrier-based aviation is concerned, the only modern type in service is the Lockheed S-3, which has advanced electronics and large weapon capability packed into a small airframe powered by two turbofans.

Helicopters are also used extensively by the military, the main roles being movement of troops and relatively light supplies, and naval tasks such as anti-submarine warfare from smaller warships. There are of course a host of other types that cannot be discussed in any detail in so

187

short a compass. Notable among these are trainers and reconnaissance
aircraft, the latter including the legendary Lockheed U-2 (and its TR-1
modern equivalent) as well as the ultimate Lockheed SR-71 'Blackbird'.

Technical advances at the present are moving swiftly, and the next
generation of aircraft will be marked by a huge leap in capability as a

*At the interface between aircraft and
space technology is the Rockwell
Shuttle Orbiter, an aerospaceplane
designed for vertical launch into space
on the power of its own main engines
(supported by two jettisonable solid-
rocket boosters), and then a gliding
return to Earth on conclusion of its
mission.*

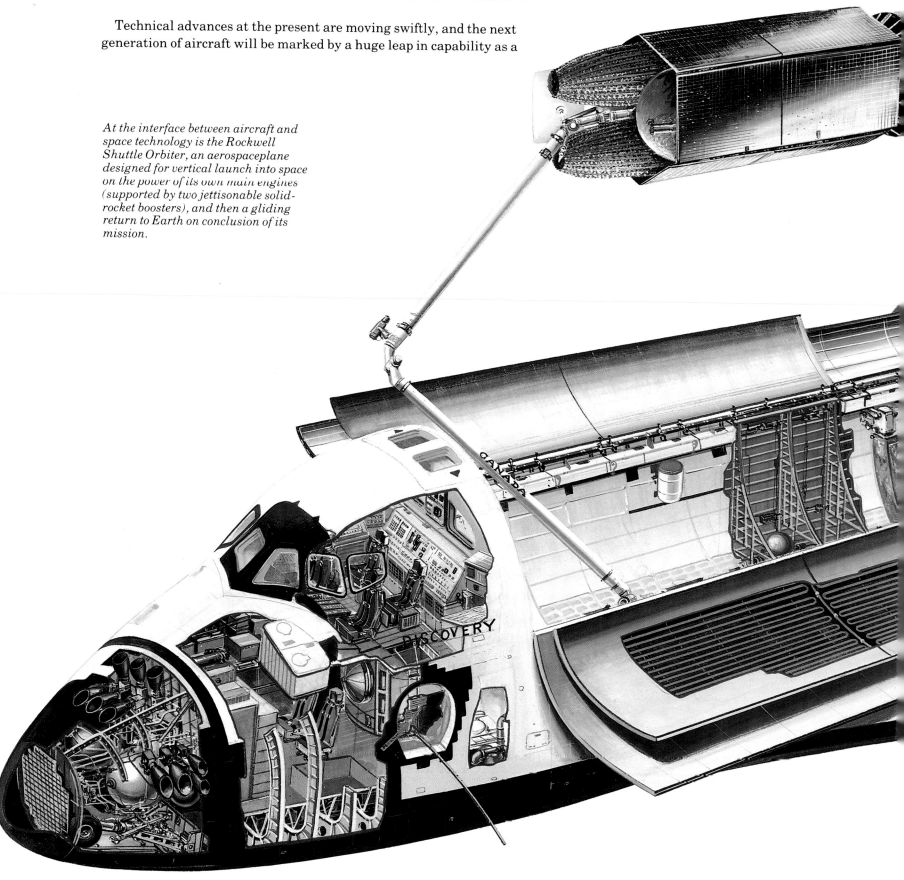

result of composite structures, engines with ceramic turbine blades, advanced aerodynamics, more sophisticated sensors of the non-emitting passive type, more capable sensors of the active type, voice-activated controls, semi-intelligent or intelligent computers, and other features to link the pilot ever more closely into the aeroplane and its systems.

Aviation has enjoyed a spectacular past and can look forward to an even more fascinating future.

189

INDEX

INDEX